Think like a GODLY man...
Act like a Virtuous Woman...

Understanding the Men of God, and Help Confirming the man that God has for your life.

T. D. Brown

Copyright © 2013 by T.D. Brown

Think like a GODLY man... Act like a Virtuous Woman...
Understanding the Men of God, and Help Confirming the man that God has for your life.

by T.D. Brown

Printed in the United States of America

ISBN 9781626976023

All rights reserved solely by the author. The author guarantees all contents are original and do not infringe upon the legal rights of any other person or work. No part of this book may be reproduced in any form without the permission of the author. The views expressed in this book are not necessarily those of the publisher.

Unless otherwise indicated, Bible quotations are taken from Amplified Bible, Old Testament, copyright © 1965, 1987 by Zondervan Corporation. New Testament, copyright 1954, 1958, 1987 by Lockman Foundation.

Kings James version, copyright 1982, by Thomas Nelson Inc.

New International Version, Copyright 1973, 1978, 1984, International Bible Society. Used By Permission of Zondervan.

Front Cover Model-Renee Singleton (Shonte Renee-Ladyrenee2011@gmail.com)-Used by permission. All rights reserved.

www.xulonpress.com

TABLE OF CONTENTS

Introduction .... *vii*

PART 1 — The Godly Man and the Virtuous Woman ..... *xv*

**Chapter 1 — Gentlemen Theory–
             Think Like a Godly Man** *16*
- *His Success* *19*
- *Relationships without Purpose* *20*

Chapter 2 — I love My Mr. Wrong *22*
- *Looks Can Be Deceiving* *23*
- *Counterfeit Impersonators* *25*
- *Why Do I Keep Meeting Mr. Wrong?* *29*
- *Embrace Your Time of Singleness* *32*
- *Never Chase a man* *33*
- *Know What You Want in Your Relationship* *36*

Chapter 3 — Holy Ghost "Hoochie Mama" *39*
- *Avoid Quick Fixes* *39*

Chapter 4 — Godly Men, Marriage, and Commitment *43*
- *I Don't Need A Man* *43*
- *You Can't Change A Man* *44*
- *Why Some Men Fear Marriage* *45*

Chapter 5 — Godly Men and Sex *48*

- Sexual Allurement 48
- Ninety-Day Rule before Sex. 50
- Sexual Attachments 52
- What You Advertise, Is What You Attract. 54

Chapter 6 — When Love Hurts — Overcoming Bad Relationships, Abuse, Hurt, and Divorce 58

- True Love. 58
- Let It Go!. 60
- Shut the Front Door! 61
- Don't Be Predictable 62
- Know Your Value 63
- Overcoming The Pain of a Bad relationship 64
- The Stages of Pain 65
- How to break-up with an Abusive Person 67
- Leave at Once 69
- Stay Away. 70
- Remain Detached. 70
  You Had To Date Them 72

Chapter 7 — Enhancing Your Marriage 74

- Godly Friends 75
- Communicate, Communicate, Communicate. 77
- Minister in Your Home First 78
- Insecurities. 79
- Swallow Your Pride 80
- Sex as a Weapon 80
- Be Sexually Creative 81
- Be Patient with Each Other During Hard Times. . . . 82
- You Hurt My Feelings 83
- Love and Listen 84
- Never Stop Dating 85
- Never Nag 86
- Value Your Relationship. 87
- Never Give Up 88
- Remain a Power Couple. 89

Table of Contents

- Plan Quality Time 90

Chapter 8 — Virtuous Women Rock! 91

PART 2 — Blueberry Letters: Real Talk About
        Relationships ... Practical, Godly Advice 97

Chapter 9 — Why do I Always Attract the
        Wrong Type of Man? 98

Chapter 10 — Divorce or Not-Married but Depressed .. 105

Chapter 11 — Cougars and Sugar Daddies 109

Chapter 12 — Abortion 111

Chapter 13 — Overcoming Molestation 113

Chapter 14 — I Want My Man to Be Happy
    —My man doesn't seem Interested 117

Chapter 15 — One-Sided Attractions 120

Chapter 16 — My Baby's Daddy Is Crazy 126

Chapter 17 — Overcoming Low-Self-Esteem 128

Chapter 18 — Overcoming Trust Issues 128

Chapter 19 — Overcoming Marriage Burn-Out 135

Chapter 20 — Overcoming Domestic Violence 139

Chapter 21 — Raise the Standard 143

Chapter 22 — He and I — and the Baby 145

Chapter 23 — Relationship Tips 147

Dedication 153
Acknowledgments 155
About The Author 156

INTRODUCTION

Dear "Eve", know that there is an "Adam" that needs YOU!

𝒢rasping for a starting point, I prayed and asked God to reveal some of the answer to me about the high divorce rate and the declining of committed relationships in this generation. Being a Godly man, I have seen far too many beautiful, rhapsodic relationships that ended horrendously. Because the reality is, we live in a shallow world and many people's interest come with motives other than love. Often times we love all the wrong people and ignore all the right people. Satisfying our eyes, and neglecting our souls. You should love hard, but pray even harder. Your footsteps need to be ordered even when you give your heart in relationships. So my perspective is not just about the relationship of marriage, but on the challenges of responsible dating also. If you're going to love smart, then you're going to have to date smart, release and detach from every person, every relationship, and every situation that no longer serves a divine purpose in your life. Many relationships have eroded because the people involved thought that they could date wrong and marry right. Even though sometimes people do change, more often than not-it's after you've been hurt many times in the process. It shouldn't take you being hurt or them getting caught for a person to want to treat you better in a relationship. I know more times than not, you can be in a relationship for years and not be happy, having to deal with domestic violence, infidelity, verbal and emotional abuse; and having to face the consequences of not thinking through the decision to engage in the relationship holistically, carefully, and prayerfully. It shouldn't take you being hurt or them getting caught for a person to want to treat you better in a relationship. In my twenty years in marriage and ministry, I have seen relationships go from heinous to admirable just from the shift of perspective, patience, and prayer. The seemingly blessedness of love leaves us with such jubilance and blinds us to the realities that relationships consist of; that is, sacrifice, submission, loyalty, and commitment.

You must be as deliberate in making a decision to engage in a relationship, as you are when buying your first home. You must be prayerful, logical, thoughtful, and willing to commit to your decision for as long as it takes. This is what a Godly man wants to know if you are willing to commit. This is what I want to explore with you in this book. Your relationship will be as strong as the knowledge you have about your man. Cheer up! There's hope — there are still godly men available and seeking you even as you read this book. Regardless of what you have read, heard, or experienced, all men are not dogs, and we don't all think exactly alike. So have the confidence, faith, and fortitude that will allow you to love yourself, be yourself, and enjoy fulfilling your God-inspired relationship.

It's all about how much you know about the way that a godly man thinks. God says, "My people shall perish for lack of knowledge" (Hos. 4:6). I do believe that same knowledge is needed in relationships as well as other areas of our lives. I'm asking that you share some of your valuable time with me in this book in order to understand with clarity how a Godly man

Introduction

thinks, how to identify him, and how to apply this information in your relationships. You'll understand that the meaning of a God-fearing man (Godly-Man) goes way beyond just going to church and a God fearing man thinks about seven critical components in a relationship: (1) He wants a woman who displays confidence. (2) He wants a woman who acts like a lady, with an open mind in intimacy. (3) He wants a woman who has initiative and takes responsibility. (4) He wants a woman who is emotionally stable. (5) He wants a woman who has good hygiene and is organized. (6) He wants a woman who is committed to God and God fearing. (7) He wants a woman who is virtuous and will cover him in prayer.

Always read the fine print. It's written in a man's character.

How a God-Fearing man thinks and his selection process of a wife is the core of this book; any man can provide financially, but it takes a Godly man to hold you up mentally, emotionally and spiritually. I will share some of the characteristics that can guide you as a virtuous woman so that you will be able to position yourself that you may be found (Prov. 18:22). My goal is to illuminate behavior, ideas, and concepts of the Godly man so you will be able to make better relational decisions and have confidence in identifying who is ultimately your God-sent soul mate.

Believe me, I get it. You are tired of all the scheming, games, and paranoia that go on in relationships. Struggling to control your feelings because they don't strategically fit with the timing God has for your life, having the feelings but not being able to express them until after the other person does for fear of losing relationship-positioning leverage, the lying, and the deception are just a nuisance. However, when you try to force the relationship or them to love you, you make it nearly impossible for them to truly love you.

I understand why many women find it difficult to trust men. Because some men don't want a good mate, they just want a good time. When you are impatient and can't wait on God's timing, that's exactly what you get; unfortunately it comes with a bad after taste. If it's your desire to be married, you need to wait for someone who is ready to be married. If you have to pressure him into doing anything that'll make you happy, he won't do it for long. Don't go dating men who just want to kick it with a friend with marriage benefits. Some men are liars, cheaters, and emotionally manipulative, a lot of men only want sex and no commitment, some just want a commitment to sex. What is worse is that many won't just let you know that, but they will try to trap or trick you into that situation. I get it. But you must remember-you attract who you are-"Men are not all the same" "Women are not all the same"; NO you're just dating the same spirit over and over again, in different bodies.

It's sad to say, but a lot of men hate to admit that they need you and don't want to see you change for the better, especially if what you used to do provided them pleasure. Pay attention to the signs early. "Yield" yourself to God. "Stop" if He says stop. "Go" if He says "go." "Turn around" if He tells you it's a dead end. When the possibility exists of someone manipulating your emotions to get what they want under false pretenses, what other choice is there but to approach relationships with caution and for your heart to be guarded? (See Proverbs 4:23.) Of course, you should be wary about how and when you express yourself, if doing so could be detrimental to your emotional and sometimes physical well-being. Sometimes women hide sensitive, personal experiences that really helped mold who they are out

Introduction

of caution that an insensitive, man will hurt them; by using that very same information or just being totally insensitive and uncaring about what they went through.

Last week a young man asked me, "Why is it so hard for my lady to trust me when I haven't done anything wrong"? I said, "I wish I had all of the answers to share with men, to help them understand why many women find it difficult to trust men and sometimes have to guard their hearts [often overly so], and why women stay on high alert." I shared the fact that somebody else may have done wrong to the woman or somebody close to her and has already rubbed her the wrong way. After all "fool me once...," right?

When was the last time you asked God for direction concerning your relationship?

I've heard many people say "I'm going to wait for whatever God has for me", and what God had for them was waiting for them to receive it. Unfortunately, they couldn't see pass the "game" or insincerity of the man and often defenses are put up to prevent pain, but they also prevent intimacy and trust. Because women are so leery about letting out sensitive information, men have to try and guess why certain things they may unknowingly ruining the trust with a woman. The women can't trust that the men are being open and honest because the likelihood of them hiding, withholding, editing, altering, or straight up lying about the truth about themselves is always in the back of the women's minds.

Many of those relationships are so easily torn apart because the foundation isn't love. There's nothing there to hold it together. At some point you must realize that; how good your mate looks or how great they are in bed is not enough to keep the relationship going strong, trials are going to come and you will need *LOVE*. A lot of women's tolerance for disrespect and commitment is based on the depth of a man's wallet, public stature: and they want commitment in marriage, regardless of whether or not that is what the man wants. Many will not admit that they need to be delivered from the "I just want to be married at any cost" spirit or the "idea of marriage." They don't always exit the relationship as soon as a man lets them know that commitment is not what he wants. Instead, a lot of women try to manipulate and change that man into what she wants. This comes off as conniving and sneaky to a man. You may have wishful thinking, but it doesn't matter how hard you push; the relationship will not go anywhere if he has told you he's not ready for commitment. *Deliverance doesn't come over night, but it never comes as long as you are in denial.* You must learn to tell yourself "no" to what you want at times; sometimes we want the wrong things or people. When you insist on pushing this type of relationship, it's as if you are saying, "God, this person came into my life by accident, and I'm going to make them stay on purpose." When, you get attached to someone who has no feelings for you. You're setting yourself up for heartache. Many women have been falling in lust all their lives, and telling the world that "Love Hurts." When what they experienced, never was love at all.

Both genders have to worry about various situations of infidelity and cheating with the other. This leads to concerns of secret lives, pregnancies, STDs, and distractions from God's purpose in life. Of course, it's hard to trust someone to be your mate when you know that there is a very real potential to be hurt emotionally, physically, and in some cases, literally killed, as a result of deception from them. Like many women who carry around emotional baggage from their past, there are many men who do the same. That "Godly" man may be having a hard time getting out of his own way and conquering his fear of being vulnerable in a relationship. Though I do believe many men simply use this reason as a cop-out and a way to deflect the real reasons, I still feel there are many who struggle with this and begin to harden their hearts and then grow cold to love. We don't always want the relationship that's best or right for us; we want what feels good. This is one of the reasons why God tells us not to be anxious for anything, including relationships (Phil. 4:6), but to pray, be honest, be loyal, court, date, but wait until you are married to be intimate.

Ultimately, a lot of women can't trust men; likewise, a lot of men can't trust women. That is mainly because men and women have hurt each other and maybe is why this issue will never come to a complete resolution. But I just wish the cycle would end and everybody would just be real and tell the person when they don't desire a committed relationship. We all must be truthful, respect each other, and seek God before getting into a relationship; if so, then we will not have to seek Him to get out of it. I'm not faulting one gender alone, but people in general. *Both* women and men have collaborated to make today's dating scene one filled with danger, abuse, lies, fear, caution, regret, insecurity, and manipulation. I do realize that a lot of the advice in this book is easier said than done; remember, It's a process. You have to work at it one day at a time. Don't get discouraged. Everybody may not be into having a committed relationship, but this book is for the woman who *IS*.

Part 1

THE GODLY MAN AND THE VIRTUOUS WOMAN

Chapter 1

Think like a Godly Man

*O*ne of the greatest misconceptions out there is that all men think the same way. There are men of every ethnicity, race, and religion who are averse to monogamous relationships, and there are men of every country, creed, and culture who are unfaithful and exhibit selfish behavior. However, we don't all think alike. There *are* men who want to be in committed relationships; believe it or not, men want to feel loved just as much as women. In some cases, it's when he doesn't feel appreciated, valued, or respected that he avoids the commitment in the relationship. I think the reason it is presumed that most men do not think this way and that most men behave this way is by and large because of stereotypes. While there is some truth to men having a common drive, how we think is based on a lot of variables like our childhood, demographics, size of the household, and where we were raised. For example, a man from the North and a man from the South or even from the Midwest may have some of the same drives, but we in essence do not think they are the same.

A Godly man and an ungodly man think totally differently. Even though name, fame, and status do play a part in

Chapter 1

whom we are, but they're not the totality of our manhood. This type of success does not bring personal fulfillment in the Godly man's life; at the end of the day, he longs to fulfill his purpose more than anything else. His purpose in the family, the job, and even friendships — he finds a way to connect it all back to God's purpose for his life. To demonstrate even more complexity, once a man finds his identity in God, his values, standards, and the way he processes his thoughts all change. He is *not* driven by sex, but now driven by what he is passionate about. He is not motivated by money alone; money now is just a means to monitor the process. Passion for God motivates Godly men — period.

Once he finds his passion, it's like he then receives a completely different DNA; he is now driven by destiny, purpose, and passion. We are not *all* trying to chase status, position, and money. While I will agree that a man is incomplete if he has no job, no place to live, or doesn't know his purpose, you must realize to really reach the core of a man, you must understand that he is a three-part being — physical, emotional, and spiritual. To him, a pocket full of money doesn't spell rich. A man, whose faith and spiritual-being positions him to never be without, spells rich. No matter what he accomplishes in the natural, be it cars, houses, money, or even a woman, he will not be fulfilled until he finds his purpose and the purpose of those things. This is one of the reasons he seems to be unstable sometimes in relationships, because if he cannot associate the relationship to his destiny, then he will be second-guessing himself and the relationship, from a spiritual point of view. As Godly men, our actions and communications must fit the God's desires for the woman we meet.

From the beginning of time when God created Adam, and once he sinned and was disconnected from God, man has longed to restore that relationship. His innate desire is to fulfill the five things God instructed him to do in the garden: (1) provide, (2) protect, (3) teach, (4) lead, and (5) cultivate. His focus will always remain on "how do I fulfill the purpose on my life?" So he begins to try to align his life first with the will of God, then with everything that he believes God has ordained to be included in his destiny. And until he finds that alignment, he realizes that his focus can't be on a woman, because he understands that until he can establish a relationship with God, all other relationships will be incomplete. So even though he may date a woman, he is praying for confirmation from God about her being that divine wife and helpmate, knowing that the favor of God is connected to the woman he meets (Prov. 18:22). I'm not saying that this is a long drawn-out process. Sometimes it is as soon as days or months, but it can be years. He is not seeking someone who is perfect or without faults, but a woman who has integrity and is on the same level of spiritual discipline that he is, a woman who can help to bring order to his life and help him to complete the transition from thinking like the average man — how much money he has, status quo, and proving his manhood — into the man that God has created him to be.

My life kind of transpired that way. My life seemed to be going well to all of the people around me, even my family. I had a very good and stable job, a top-of-the-line automobile, and I had every title and accolade that you could think of, but still I lacked fulfillment as a man. I knew there had to be more to life than the materialistic things and just being in a relationship just to say I had somebody to love me. I felt very empty inside and didn't really know what it was that I should seek, but I knew there was something that I was missing. I dated, I bought a new car almost every year, and I had many friends; but I was still confused about my purpose and destiny. I wanted to settle down but couldn't find the person

Chapter 1

who understood exactly what I was feeling. I didn't want just another date or just another relationship; I desired to have the one God had designed for me.

I began to pray for my soul mate, and God said to me, "A soul mate is not one particular person, but a *type* of spirit." After praying, I was out riding with one of my friends, and a woman that I had spoken with a year prior came up to my car in the parking lot and befriended me. She began to ask me a strange question: "How can I improve your quality of life?" As corny as it may sound, that was the million-dollar question, because it sparked a light in me, causing me to realize that she understood the first need of a Godly man. A woman must be able to cultivate a man's spirituality and supplement who he is in God and be a helper to him, fulfilling the calling of manhood on his and her life.

A Godly man is held more accountable for his actions and his words because he is more knowledgeable of God's truths and commands. He is always in constant pursuit of his God-given destiny. If he's not pursuing his "destiny," "purpose," and "God's will for his life," he's incomplete and has a hard time facing that reality and conveying that to his significant other. Many ladies have asked me, "Why does it seem like he is not into me?" You must realize that until a man discovers his purpose, he really can't understand his existence because he must realize that cars, houses, money, and status can't fulfill him. Finding his purpose is the only way to fulfillment.

His Success

Most men regardless of their backgrounds or religious beliefs want to be Mr. Right, they are looking for love; whether they admit it or not. Some just aren't ready to receive it. With all of the distractions and pressures of the world, some find themselves confused by lust and living contrary to who they really are. By defining success based on what others assume to be success; and usually this is where what he is doing, does not match who he really is. One of the first questions that a woman should ask a man is, "Do you understand your purpose?" and "What is your perspective of the purpose of this relationship?" and then really listen to how he answers those two questions. This will contribute to her understanding and happiness as well.

Relationships without Purpose

Courting for marriage- is not the same as dating for pleasure.

While giving your time during the dating phase, you are giving them a portion of your life that you will never get back. Don't be afraid of losing someone who isn't going to be in your life for a purpose. A relationship without purpose is an experiment that will lead to frustration, hurt, disappointment, and a waste of time. Without defining and committing to the purpose of the relationship, it will only be a trial-and-error event, with a good chance that there will be no success. See; when you keep dating to gain nothing, you always lose something; you lose time; you lose hope in what's real; and when you lose these things, dating has officially started to bring death to you in some form. Until you are ready to admit to yourself exactly what it is that you want, you will experience relationship confusion.

You must date with purpose! Some women are single because they are too quick to invest all of themselves into short term relationships. If marriage isn't the purpose, there is no real purpose. This is the reason for so many heart breaks. Even now, when I wake up in the morning, with all

Chapter 1

of the materialistic things one can have, I am still in pursuit of purpose. A Godly man can have all the tangibles, from the nice house with the picket fence, to many cars in his garage and being able to provide and protect his family; but still realize that all that does not quantify him as a man. He seeks to confirm why he exists and that the relationship is not just a coincidence. He struggles with Matthew 6:33, seeking the kingdom of God (God's purpose for his life), because he knows there is much more to life than those things. This is very important in a relationship because he will not be fulfilled until he is at least headed in the right direction and hears the call of God on his life. So ladies, don't beat yourself up thinking something is wrong with you or you are not good enough. You must know that the struggle for success is not about you, but within him.

Chapter 2

I Love My Mr. Wrong

You can't expect a Bad boy… not to treat you Bad.

Don't confuse feelings for facts!!...because you feel like he's the right one, doesn't mean he is the God sent one! The man or woman God has for you could be found in a type you never considered. If you knew how to choose your type, maybe you wouldn't have had as many broken relationships or you'd be married by now. A lot of folks will tell you "I'm waiting for whatever God has for me" and are rejecting what He's trying to give them at the same time. God wouldn't send someone to love you part-time or seasonal. Someone who doesn't see the value in you being a part of their life won't really make the efforts, to keep you there. The man for you should be there to stay and will display commitment qualities. As always, God has given you your woman's intuition, and when men approach you, naturally you will utilize it; but most importantly, seek God for discernment- "You have to trust God more than you trust you." Your intuition is not accurate all of the time. Don't try to be what you "think" someone is going to like. Instead, be who God says you are, and He'll show you who you were made to be with. You must not operate from pure emotions alone while waiting on God to send your soul mate (that is, loneliness, raging hormones, family pressure, and biological clock); you must remove any of these distractions from your life and willfully open your ear to the Lord. If not, you will not be able to discern the "church players." A man in the church doesn't always mean he's a man in Christ; and doesn't always mean he's the man for you.

Not long ago a woman thought she had met her God-ordained husband in the church; five months later in a routine yearly medical checkup, she discovered she was HIV positive. It seems that her God-ordained husband was a down-low (DL) brother, having unprotected sexual infidelity relationships with both men and women and had full-blown AIDS, which he knew when he married her. Everything that glitters isn't gold (Matt 7:15). Just because a man is popular and in church does not necessarily mean he is sent from God! It would be wise of you to learn to use your discernment.

Looks Can Be Deceiving

1 John 4:1(Message) My dear friends, don't believe everything you hear. Carefully weigh and examine what people tell you. Not everyone who talks about God comes from God. There are a lot of lying spirits loose in the world.

Men know men; we can identify with why so many men are attracted to a woman; therefore we observe how she responds to the attention. You really have to observe a man's actions, and his spirit. Don't go off words alone. If you can't identify a person by their spirit, you don't really know who you're dealing with (1Jn 4:1).

The Word states "you will know him by his *fruits* (Matt 7:16)." Just because a man looks like he has it all together, be careful, because sometimes he is the one with more issues than anyone else. The mouth can say "I'm an educated, humble, church going man" and their spirit can be screaming "I'm a lustful, prideful lover of pleasure." You can discern Mr. Wrong by his conversation. First of all, he will start out talking spiritually; this usually lasts about a month or two. Then his conversation will become carnal (materialistic), and his attention and focus will shift to the physical (your body). Ladies, let's be honest. A bad boy is not looking for a good woman; he's bad for a reason. You know it, and he knows it. Stop ignoring this fact. Typically, when it comes to intimacy, he will begin to say things like, "One time will not hurt anybody"; and "God understands, He knows we are not perfect." Every man knows that most single women of God are waiting for their Bo-Az, to come and sweep them off their feet. As a woman, you can't have a Jezebel spirit (low standards) and be waiting for your Boaz; Jezebel didn't have a Boaz

Then Bo-Az announced to the elders and all the people, "Today you are witnesses that I have bought from Naomi all the property of Elimelek, Kilion and Mahlon. I have also acquired Ruth the Moabite, Mahlon's widow, as my wife, in order to maintain the name of the dead with his property, so that his name will not disappear from among his family or from his hometown. Today you are witnesses!" – Ruth 4:9-10; see also verses 11-13

So while waiting on your Bo-Az; that is, Mr. Right, you have to be able to recognize his;

Chapter 2

Counterfeit Impersonators

This is Key—The closer you get to God, the clearer you can see the devil. If you can't see the devil, you'll date a whole lot of them.

First, there is *Married-Az*. He smiles all the time. He's the one who, even though he attends church, pretends he is not in a relationship or married. Some of the telltale signs are that he doesn't want to meet your friends in the church, he doesn't introduce you to his friends, or he never fellowships after church with the leaders because he does not want them asking too many questions that might reveal his hidden agenda. This man usually has money and will try to control and lock you down into a commitment, though he never has intentions of being faithful or leaving his wife to be with you. Even though he has someone, he is still too insecure and selfish to allow you to date other people, even though he's married. He promises you a committed relationship with security and monogamy but is just keeping you around as a side chick for his convenience.

Lying-Az: In the majority of his conversation, he boasts about what he has and his past accomplishments, but nothing can be verified or proven. Always boasting about he's a real man, real men have no need to tell you they are real. He talks a good game, but when things don't go the way he wants them to, he changes like a lizard with many shades of colors and with a personality to match. This guy is sweet, articulate, intellectual, sensitive, emotional, and shows respect for women. The thing is, he usually will insult or put down other guys to show that he is better than the typical guy. In the end, all he wants to do is have sex with you and be gone. You will see a sharp 180-degree turn right after he has sex with you. This guy will say all the right things, like beautiful quotes and poetry on his Facebook statuses. He will create a fake world that surrounds him and his accomplishments on social networks, usually because he's not really happy with his real life; or could be sending signals to his Ex, trying to pretend that things are bigger, and better than what they really are. So, be prayerful dating people from social network cites who don't like who they are; as they will lie about their identity in virtual space, because it doesn't match who they are in real life!

Cheatin-Az: This Mr. Wrong is very deceiving and can really cause grave danger to your heart and mind. He typically starts the conversation on a spiritual basis; he will quote a few scriptures to entice you to let your guard down. He will invite you to spend time with him, but only in private places. He may even invite you to go on trips, but usually the place that is recommended is isolated or away from the city. His goal is to sustain two or more relationships while keeping them parallel to each other. Don't be deceived by his knowledge of Scripture because Scripture is used as the old "bait and reel" tactic.

He knows you are seeking a closer walk with God, and he will play on that very fact. So he will quote scriptures like, "I'm Bo-az looking for my Ruth"; or "The Bible says a man who finds a wife finds a good thing. I'm looking for my wife." He understands that these words will draw most spiritual women in and make them very vulnerable.

Lazy-Az. This man will sell you a dream of the future but knows he will never live up to it. He promises marriage, a white house with a picket fence, kids, and the fairy tale. He says it will come as soon as he makes it in the "rap game, producer, Med school, etc." or you can insert any unrealistic dream where he makes it big. He is usually a mama's boy or has mama issues. His mama cooked, cleaned, did his laundry, and spoiled him, so he's not used to taking care of himself. This guy always keeps a girlfriend but is never faithful. He hates being alone, so he will always have some nurturing female on lockdown. Don't feel bad if you have fallen victim to one of these guys, for they are professional liars. Unfortunately, in this generation, some men don't like responsibility and don't know what it means to do things for themselves. They were either babied or spoiled as a child by their mama with an absentee father, or they are just plain lazy. You don't work, you don't eat — plain and simple (2 Thess. 3:10). You have to be candid and stern with this type of man in the very beginning because you are about to set the tone for the relationship. Whatever you accept now will be hard to change later. *This type of man will begin to think in his mind that you desire to take care of him.*

Some men know how to pick out women who they know will take care of them. Typically, this man will pick up on a woman's low self-esteem and begin to spend time with her, only to use her for her money, home, car, or sex. I have always wondered if this kind of woman has an invisible sign on her head that only these men can see, because I have met many men who always have a woman taking care of them. He is not lazy, in that he does have a job, but he is always living with some woman. These are women with decent jobs who appear to have sense, but I guess at the end of the day, a man will only do what he is allowed. Basically, the man that you allow to use you in this capacity feels like he is doing his part in the relationship because he feels that you are lonely and insecure, and his spending time with you will balance your needs as well as his.

Ladies, Take your time. If a man is really interested, he will not be in a hurry. You must realize you cannot buy a man — period.

When you are that desperate just to have a man, it turns him off more than anything else. He will begin to push away from you over time and at some point start resisting your money. Though it started out as something new, now he is not attracted to you any longer because your eagerness to take care of him has become a turnoff. Real simple, virtuous women don't take care of grown men. If he doesn't work, he shouldn't eat (2 Thes. 3:10). Working hard is mandatory. If he won't work hard to support himself, he won't work hard to support you.

User-Az: This guy will take advantage of a woman's motherly instincts and desire to help a man out. He will use her for money, her car, and a place to stay. This guy usually will pretend to fall in love within the first week to a month. He then will try to move in as soon as you accept the "love" he is offering you. He will use whatever tools he can to control your emotions and make you tied to taking care of him. When you try to leave him, he will make it seem as if you are wrong for throwing a man in need on the street. This guy can be dangerous at times. He will target your self-esteem by calling you ugly and make it seem as if no other man wants you. These men are prone to violence and will make you feel trapped mentally and physically.

Lusting-Az: This guy usually has three or more baby mamas and will lock himself to you by impregnating you. This guy quite obviously has the spirit of lust, but for some reason, women fall for him. He usually gives himself away by mentioning how you will give him "pretty kids" or that he wants you to have his baby. This guy is usually a pretty boy or a thugged-out ladies' man. Once you become his baby mama, he will become a leech/user and take advantage of the fact that you don't want to be a single mother and will do whatever it takes to not be a baby mama, and raise your kid(s) by yourself.

Chapter 2

His self-esteem and manhood are based on how many chicks he has had sex with or can pull to him. He has no pride in himself; the goal is to have sex by any means necessary. He shares several traits with the other guys on the list and always brags about how he pulls the "baddest" chicks. He just wants to add you to his long list of baby mamas. Use your discernment and fade away from this type of man — fast! (See 1 Corinthians 6:18.)

At times, he will even try to draw you in with gifts, rings, purses, or even a car. You cannot allow a person to use their resources to use you or cloud your judgment. They will flaunt them when they desire to sleep with you, then they fade-out, and when you get fed up, and they reel you back with gifts... Don't get so hype over these gifts that you miss their actions; and begin to put a price tag on your temple. Read between the lines... It doesn't matter how nice or expensive the gift is, if they aren't paying attention any other time; that's cuffing, not appreciation.....You don't have to be standing on a corner to be prostituting, sex appeal will get you gifts and great sex, but doesn't promise you a great mate. Get substance or get laid. The choice is yours....

Why Do I Keep Meeting Mr. Wrong?

When choosing a mate, just because the frame is different doesn't mean the spirit is different. You must stop choosing different frames, and dating the same ungodly spirit. Maybe you keep meeting Mr. Wrong simply because they are not ready for Mrs. Right; and the readiness is yet to come, because you are not making the necessary changes in your character when it comes to your values, standards, and dignity. Self-value is a must, value yourself enough to choose to be with someone, who wants you as much as you want them. When you meet a person you are interested in-present your sincere self and give yourself time to gauge his sincerity; getting to know them will be a process, don't be so hasty to "act" married with someone you aren't married to. The way a man treats you is directly indicative of how he really feels about you and how you feel about yourself. Now, when I say "treats" I don't mean the compliments he gives you, or the places he takes you out to eat, or some other innocuous or superficial treatment. When I say 'the way a man treats you', it's about how much of his life does he let you in. How much of his soul does he let you see, how much does he truthfully share. If you feel like he's treating you like a jump-off or a friend with benefits, it's probably because that's exactly what you are to him. If you don't want that, then you better guard your heart until God confirms the relationship. Part of your frustration may be that you don't realize there are some men who don't have the capacity to know how to receive your love; some men just can't give you what they don't have. Your definition of quality is written all over the type of people you choose to date; who else is there to blame for you choosing to date someone who doesn't possess any of the character traits you say you want in a mate? Sometimes we simply make bad investments. Chalk up your losses, take the lesson and move forward. It's not always that you made the wrong choice; sometimes two people are in the right situation but doing things the wrong way. Like lowering your standards just to date someone, therefore allowing the people who you are trying to please, to dictate your standards. Just give people the real you–Being real is about being true to who you are, and standing on what you believe in. Be confident in you. Make sure you're not openly inviting the attention you say you don't want. "Loving smart" means believing in yourself, your worth, and your value. We can't see ourselves blocking our own blessings. Being who God wants you to be, has to become more important than who you're trying to be for a man.

Chapter 2

Being kept by God- will make you a keeper!

Why do we fall for someone, who really isn't for us? Many ladies often zoom in on the idea of being in a relationship with a man, before the man has made his intentions clear, which leads to premature emotional commitment; when all the man wanted was a friend with benefits. Should we blame ourselves for falling for the wrong one or should we blame the one we fell for? Have you ever considered that; good relationships fall apart so a better relationship can fall together? Every story has an end, but in life every end is just a new beginning. Some relationships don't work out, and they leave you feeling lonely because you were probably led by your emotions or a person instead of being led by God. The problem is lack of patience, and discipline. Not wanting to take the time to establish your-self in Christ before seeking a mate. Attempt to make sure you're relationship with God is right and He'll make sure you're in the right relationships-being treated right. God loves you so much....there are some people he won't even allow you to date successfully. He never allows a relationship that replaces Him to last long when you are a child of God. But, He "Will allow the wrong relationship choices to bring us to the right places with Him and our destiny." Any person you marry outside the will of God is called a "distraction." You can avoid a lot of these distractions by not putting your hope in a potential relationship with someone who still entertains the possibility of being with someone else; and not entering a relationship with a person simply for a vested interest, or because he is convenient. For all those women who say, "All men are the same," well, God never told you to try them all! Allow God to bring a real, Godly man into your life.

Embrace Your Time of Singleness

Learning how to be faithfully single will help you become a faithful companion.

Friends and family unknowingly will place pressure on you during your singleness; asking and wondering why you are not dating someone; contrary to what you might believe, this is a good time to work on your inner-self and get closer to God. Do not allow others to make you feel embarrassed about being single. There is no shame in following God's plan and timing for YOUR life. This sometimes requires a willingness to put people, places and things on hold, and sometimes; even out of sight, as you spend time in prayer. Trust in God. He will not have you ignorant to what precautions you are to take and whom you are to date (Rom. 1:13). Be sure to Seek Him more than you seek them. If someone else is responsible for making you happy, they also have the power to make you miserable. Happiness is to be shared with a mate, but it should never revolve around anyone. You must know your worth ladies. You can't be sold once you really understand that you've already been bought with a price (1Cor 6:20). Use your singleness as a tool to improve yourself for you and for your future spouse. Don't allow this time of being single to become loneliness and do not allow it to devour your happiness because you are not in a relationship. When it's time to commit, you may not be perfect but you should be fit for the relationship. There's no time like alone time. Take some time to learn and exercise what's right for your life before trying to invite someone else to share it with. Time for you to communicate privately with the Lord; it'll teach you about you, and how to deal with others. Most women are not content with their singleness and are desperate for marriage. You must embrace your time of singleness and find happiness within you. Be secure in who you are–Other people's opinions and lies shouldn't be able to breech your confidence in the truth about you. You have to value the condition of your soul; you have to guard it, and tend to it. Love is about your soul, not your body. You're not taking care of your soul just because you look good, smell good, dress nice, or have money. None of that means you really love... you. Love, peace, joy, wisdom, faith, etc...These are the things your soul needs. You have to make room. Evict the pride, lusts, lies, low self-esteem, etc. If you can't get passed your own exterior, you'll never attract someone else who can. What you're looking for in someone else, is a reflection of the way you tend to yourself.

Most of you ladies make relationship decisions based on your emotions. If not balanced, emotions can be a tool Satan uses to pollute and destroy God's purpose. Now, ladies, think about how many men you have slept with in your past on pure emotion. Emotions can lie to you. Sometimes it's better to force yourself to do what is right, even if it feels wrong. Be honest with yourself and judge yourself on the issue. You see, this is why many women have so much pain from relationships and failures in relationships; you make decisions based on pure emotion instead of listening to your born- again spirits. Most of the relationships that you have engaged in, God gave you all the red flags, but you intentionally ignored them. Don't fall into dating folks who are committed to common interests (partying, sex, money, etc) Love can't be built on any of it. In essence, if you allow God to confirm your real estate, then your relationship stands a lesser chance of going into foreclosure.

Never Chase a Man

"Don't settle for a relationship that won't let you be yourself."

If you're dating someone in a short time after your last relationship ended, you're still relationship hopping. Spend some time with God first. Then, fall in love naturally, don't force your-self to love someone out of desperation or loneliness. You don't have to run behind a man. The right man is supposed to find you, just focus on being the right woman. If your partner can't take the time to become "best friends" first in the relationship, it's best if you cut it off. The trust needs to be established. You MUST have balance... don't trust too much, don't love too much, don't hope too much. Because, too much; can hurt you so much. The type of standards you value most are evident in the type of people you date. Moral–Finance–Image–Sex.

If he's not a responsible, respectable man when you meet him; you inviting him into your life is the risk you take. If you want true love then WAIT on God! Mr. Right — he's probably right under your nose.

My number one advice to you is to stop looking so hard, and *pray*! If God placed a man in your life, you won't have to try to find him or impress him into liking you; he will love you for who you are. Be you and stop trying to pretend you don't like him because of fear. If you like him, you like him, but don't chase him; the mix signals will push him away. There are many good men out there, you have to get out of your normal routine so he can find you; but, you cannot allow your desperation to take over. You're probably giving off a "marriage, kids, *now*" vibe, and that will scare him away. If you want to settle down, you will. Keep that in mind. It *will* happen, unless God has other plans for your future. Keep in mind that your life doesn't have to operate on some imaginary deadline that you have set. While most people will tell you, "Until God sends Mr. Right, stop looking for love, and it will find you," I disagree with that. You can't take a passive role in

Chapter 2

your own life. I hate when people say, "Oh, when you're least expecting it . . ." When will that be? While I do think there is some veracity to this comment, you still must be proactive, but don't be anxious for the relationship (Phil. 4:6).

You have to realize how much God loves you. He loves you more than you could ever imagine and he wants the best for you, including your relationship. The moment you begin to realize how much God loves you, and that you don't have to prove yourself anymore, neither do you have to spend your life trying to impress a man or other people-it's an incredible deliverance. Virtuous women know who they are and do not need a relationship to validate their lives. A Godly man seeks a woman who is not only secure about the relationship with him, but is also confident of who she is in God. Men find confidence sexy and an insecure woman a turnoff. Every man finds beauty in a woman who recognizes her inner beauty (1 Pet.3:4).

Many women seek Mr. Right for the wrong reasons. You must have fun with your life and just be content with being by yourself before actually entering a relationship with this type of man. Desperation or lack of patience is a weakness, and that's one reason the Bible states, "Be anxious for nothing," because the enemy will use it against you to fall into depression, low self-esteem, etc. And most guys, if given the chance, will take advantage of that. Again, I'm not saying not to be proactive, but what I am saying is be happy with yourself *first*. Allow God to help you find different priorities, such as your future, school, long-term goals, or self-development, so you will have something to bring to the table.

Now you are ready for Mr. Right, but remember, you must be proactive, pray effectually, date graciously, and choose wisely. Even though you are not looking for him, you should still try to go out with your friends or do things solo so that you make yourself more available. Attend church regularly, join the singles group, go shopping, go to the movies, go anywhere you want. I think the more you are out of your house, the more you'll up your chances of Mr. Right introducing himself to you. Now, before the introduction, *you* need to be prepared. You must allow God to prepare you in order to have a loving, successful relationship. Maybe you have been attracting wrong people because of you; that is, hanging out at wrong places where wrong or negative people hang out, sending the wrong signals to wrong people without being aware of your own actions.

Know What You Want in Your Relationship

You have to veer from stunting your own growth. You have to deny yourself dates with people you know don't share the same goals, values and self-respect.

Remember, happiness starts with you, not with your relationship, your friends or your job; but with you. You have to be what you seek. Many women like to believe that their relationships didn't work out because their partners weren't good enough, when sometimes it's you not knowing what you want. If you want marriage; take the time and allow God to prepare you to become a wife. So, if you have been attracting the wrong people, maybe-you need to work on yourself first. There are six billion people on this earth, but somehow you manage to end up with one particularly wrong person(s) for you. You walk into a room, and you are drawn to one wrong man out of twenty right men in the room. Getting yourself ready first is crucial because if you are *not* ready to receive Mr. Right and not able to recognize Mr. Right, even several hundred right men will walk right in front of you, introduce themselves to you, and you will ignore all of them.

Then, once you are ready, take the time to write down what type of relationship you want and what you want from the relationship, and present it to God in prayer (Phil. 4:6–7). Many women do not know what they want from a relationship or what kind of relationship makes them happy. They just want a Mr. Right without understanding that Mr. Right is only half of that relationship. Without knowing what you want from and in a relationship, you do not know what Mr. Right should be like; he is only right when he is right for you, and the *relationship you expect*.

You must set boundaries.

When God is trying to show you who a person really is, don't let "your" will get in the way of seeing them for who they really are. Part of attracting the right Godly man is saying "No" when you encounter the wrong man. Set appropriate boundaries regarding respect and mistreatment to discourage undesirable men. Set clear boundaries early in the relationship so that there will be no confusion down the line about what you expect from a man. Be very honest and realistic about what you want from the relationship and what the relationship means to you. This is very important. It can be as simple as "we're both in ministry together;" "we have a house, two kids, and a dog; "we both love God more than we love each other"; "someone with the character of God"; "he supports my dreams and ambitions"; "we are good and loving parents of three loving kids"; "he loves me like Christ loved the church"; etc. Write down the values, attributes, characteristics, morals, etc. that you want Mr. Right to possess.

Include how you want him to feel towards you.

It can be many pages. Pray and meditate on the list, and keep telling yourself that you deserve and want that relationship. Now you are ready to receive Mr. Right.

God doesn't need your help in finding you a husband; He needs your willingness to let Him make you a wife. Many women ask me, "How will I know he is Mr. Right, when I meet him?" Good question. Each relationship is different, and all men do not think alike when it comes to relationships and commitment. Start by praying; just be honest and say, "It's not my time yet; I have to trust the process God has for me." Meanwhile, keep your legs closed and your mind open. Yeah, temptation is rough, but Mr. Right is not seeking a Holy Ghost Hoochie Mama. I don't mean that with any disrespect, but Mr. Right's priority will not be sex. He's not seeking just another girl to have sex with, but a woman he can marry and have sex with...the woman that understands the meaning of sex and him.

Chapter 3

Holy Ghost "Hoochie Mama"

You can't have a loose lifestyle and expect a tight relationship.

Avoid Quick Fixes

A "Holy Ghost Hoochie Mama" isn't fit for anybody. Being a "HGHM" will put you in the wrong places at the wrong time. Then, you meet the wrong people who eventually treat you the wrong way. The way a man approach you is the result of the way you present yourself. You can't take pride in being a seductress and wonder why men don't ever approach you with substance. The "bait" can't place labels on the fish; the fish is just doing what it's supposed to do; trying to eat what's on the hook... Settle down as an individual before looking for someone to settle down with. Things that used to attract and excite you should at some point begin to grieve you. It's called maturity and wisdom; Learning better, doing better. Someone who has settled down as an individual doesn't have to be in the club every night/week or must have a man to find joy. Get yourself under control. "HGHM" are usually looking for outlets to pacify the lack of peace, joy, faith, self-esteem, etc... You must realize that sometimes spending time alone is the best medicine because when you seek an outside mate to cure your loneliness on the inside, it can cause you to lower your standards. Then you will try to get-to-know the person through physical intimacy, and this will deceive you into thinking you are closer to someone than you really are. While I do agree that dating is the correct activity for getting to know someone, you must realize that it's not for sex and using a person to numb your pain or loneliness. Seeking a quick fix for your pain or damaged self-esteem can leave you branded as a "Holy Ghost hoochie mama" and leave you open to sexual and emotional manipulation.

The HGHM is a woman who goes to church regularly, but who has lowered her standards and self-respect when it comes to love. She says one thing, but her behavior is contrary to her speech. Typically, she has been hurt in a past relationship, went through a messy divorce, or has been emotionally or physically abused. She will sleep around without conviction and has low expectations from any man she dates, because of her past. Her self-esteem has been damaged, so she goes along to get along and every man she sleeps with, boost-up her esteem. Ladies, everyone gets tired of being disrespected, hearing men say lies like, "I'm sorry," but then doing the same thing again, and hurting. But don't allow your hurt to cause you to seek negative attention. Catching a man's eye is not the same as having his attention, and sharing his bed is not sharing his heart. Keeping yourself out of unhealthy environments, from unhealthy activity and communications will help you to be kept by God, remove the hurt and prepare you for your soul mate. You can't expect the person God's going to place in your life to see you as marriage material if you begin to sleep around because you're hurt. You must realize–some men chase the females who are lonely, hurt or needy and not the housewife because they want the pleasure, not the responsibility. A man's persistence will reveal one of

Chapter 3

two things. His sincere interest in being next to you OR his extreme thirst to be inside you..

Your standards are not as high as you may think they are if you're giving out marriage benefits to a single man.

The HGHMs have made it harder for women who are virtuous and walk in integrity to be able to be found by Godly, committed men. They profess to be saved, but this type of woman continues to give up the cookies (sex) mainly, to the men in the church; and when a man begins to date a virtuous woman, he assumes that she has the same standards, because of what he has experienced with the HGHMs.

Although, I believe waiting to be intimate is the Godly thing to do, it seems to be hypocritical of the truth based on this woman's behavior and habits. While the virtuous woman is implying that she would like to wait to be intimate, take things slowly, and wait for God to confirm the relationship, the HGHM is constantly giving up the cookies (sex) all the while.

The Jezebel(Un-Godly woman), is more attractive than Ruth (Godly woman) to a man who loves with his eyes.

Even though this isn't Mr. Right pursuing this type of woman, Mr. Right is looking at the situation and asking, "How do I know if this Godly woman is any different?" And the man who's in the sin with you, and playing you says in his head, "I'm going to let you pretend around your family and friends, cry, speak in tongues, and pretend like God is keeping you; but after church is dismissed and the lights go off, I know you are going to lower your standards and fall right into position." As a consequence, you have not modeled the difference between the street hoochie and the virtuous woman. So the man says in his mind, "Why should I commit? And if I do decide to settle down, why should I marry her?" You have to come to grips with the reality that a man is only going to value you as much as you value yourself. *You shouldn't be easy access to anyone. You have to grow to a level of self-respect where you're not just "somebody to date."*

Love gives, lust takes. Lust is always looking for a way to be pleased, love is always looking to enlighten, enhance, and enrich. You, when acting like a Holy Ghost hoochie mama — when he thinks about it — you and the ungodly woman have the same standards. There will be a lot of men coming to the Lord. So let's get something straight before you try to touch him; let God touch him. Before he gets to know you, let him get to know God. Before you get in his face, let him get in God's face. Stop chasing the men in the house of God. Leave that man alone and allow him to chase God without any distractions. I understand that sometimes you get lonely, your hormones are raging and your flesh gets weak, but that's where you fight. Loneliness is a spirit. Pray it out.

Ladies, the moral to this chapter is, BE RESPONSIBLE WITH YOU. Sometimes you have to stand in the mirror, stare into your soul, come to yourself and say "I'm better than this." It's time to raise the bar; up the ante...you deserve better.

Chapter 4

Godly Men, Marriage, and Commitment

Just because a man is mature-doesn't mean he's marriage ready.

Many women who have finally made it up the corporate ladder or become stable in a nice entry-level job still come home at the end of the day to a nice, pristine home, nicely decorated and full of amenities, but experience loneliness because there is no companionship there. Many women state that they can date themselves — and you should — because there are times when you find yourself staring across the table at another couple, wishing. Men view commitment differently from woman-we see it to be so final in the dating arena; and most have a hard time committing because in the back of our mind, we have to ensure you are the keeper or wife that we would like to spend the rest of our life with. If a man who LOVES you isn't ready to marry you, he won't ignore the topic; he will most likely voice his un-readiness or give you hints to be patient. If he strikes up the conversation and starts talking about the future with you, chances are he sees a future with you. This could be your clue; men don't talk marriage for fun.

I Don't Need a Man

If man didn't need woman, God wouldn't have created help for Adam. Eve wasn't a mistake and neither are you.

Then there are women who say, "I don't need a man to fulfill me." And they don't, but they find themselves taking short vacations to the Bahamas with their sisters and their mamas (I guess that's why they call it the Bahamas Mama), only to find later that's not really what they want. So they start to settle for any man who will spend time with them. They begin to date out of anxiety and now tolerate anything and everything because they feel good as long as they have a man — any man. I must warn you, if the dating relationship isn't working, don't get married thinking it'll improve. It will make the breakup expensive.

You Can't Change a Man

Until you make peace with who you are, you will never be content with who you're dating.

Love is pure (1Cor 13:4). You can't seek something pure from a man who's toxic. Going into a relationship thinking you can change a man is your first mistake. If a man wants to be married, he'll act like it. If he doesn't, he'll act like it. It's your responsibility to guard your heart from being broken and to guard your mind from being played with. Some men, in a way, are like cats. If you keep feeding him cookies, he will keep coming back, even though he is not yours. If he like doing this, that and the other, and you don't; Don't pretend to relate just because you like him. As I have said before, you can't date wrong and expect to marry right. Never go outside of yourself in attempts to be common with a man. You don't need to be common with him, you need to be you. Pray and allow God to lead you (Prov. 3:5), and abstain from sex before marriage, because sex does not equal intimacy. Sex outside of marriage reduces intimacy rather than building it. Give the relationship time to grow. The right man of God will have the same view about sex outside of marriage that God does.

Like you, most men are called to marriage.

The odds of a man being created to be celibate are pretty darn small; very few people have that gift. He may question himself, really wondering if he is called to a life of singleness. But don't let him fool you; if he has a desire for sex, then he is called to marriage at some point in his life. Speaking for myself, I never wanted to be married until I gave my life to Christ. Before then, I always felt like marriage was so final. The thought always permeates a man's mind, "Is this really the person I want to spend the rest of my life with?"

Then God touched my life, and now I wanted to focus on the purpose and destiny God had on my life, and that included the woman for me. Once I received salvation, I wanted marriage badly. I basically said, "Okay, God, I really want this, but if You want me to remain single, I'll remain single." I totally gave up marriage in my heart. At this point, God spoke to me and said, "It's just working in My timing, not yours." If you want it, you are called to it, but enjoy your single life secure in the knowledge that someday it will happen. Just focus on making yourself the type of person that the husband you are looking for is expecting. I was courting my soon-to-be wife at the time, and then I was engaged three months later. It was totally a God thing, and well, it was *His* timing, not mine!

Why Some Men Fear Marriage

u do NOT want a man who doesn't have a fear ... and a Husband spirit. God wants to send you a husband; You don't need to figure out how to be a good girlfriend.

Real Men-get Married, Men Of God-stay Married. What does a Godly man truly fear about getting married? Is it the idea of intimacy that marriage brings? No. I adore having a significant other with whom I can share my innermost thoughts and feelings. Is it the loss of romantic freedom? No. I was by nature monogamous, and I don't have any issue committing myself to a single woman. Honestly, it's the fact that once he commits, the reality is that this is the last woman he will have a chance to be with. So he reasons within himself, "Am I sure this is the last cookie in the box, or should I wait on the next one? Is this woman good for me now, but will she be controlling and possessive later? Will she keep herself up physically and morally? Will I regret this decision later?"

Chances are, he has been exposed to marriages featuring men and women who stick together; not because they want to, not because they have any real affection for each other, but because they are entangled by their circumstances, be it children, shared property, financial commitments, etc. He doesn't want that to be his life. He says in his mind, "If I am going to get married, I want to be with a woman I enjoy being with, and I want to perpetually enjoy being with her."

So, during the courting phase, you have to get him to be explicit about what his needs are to be happy in a relationship. You and he will have to be aware of each other's deepest requirements for a stable relationship; the ones that we create consciously, and the ones that we don't, but are there regardless. For example, I have to understand that my wife Tammy

Chapter 4

prefers social activities with other people, not just sitting at home with me all the time.

Then there are men who avoid accountability; they want their women to be committed, but they want to be able to go and do as they please. Ladies, you have to allow God to raise the standard (Isa. 59:19) in this area of your life; because a man will see how much of your everything he can get without giving up anything. He may visit your family, socialize, and even attend your kids' activities, but will not invite you to visit his family. If you allow him to continue to do this, it will become a turnoff to him because this exudes a woman of low-self esteem, one who is willing to give up her life to a man without a commitment. A Godly man will not commit himself to a woman who is not committed to herself and to God. In summary, all I'm saying is live your life. Don't spend all your time waiting for that next relationship or worrying about whether your current relationship will lead to marriage. A Godly man will be attracted to a Godly woman who has a full lively life, established goals, outside of her relationship with a man.

Chapter 5

Godly Men and Sex

*E*ven when it's come to sexual relations in marriage, some Godly men have no clue on how to sexually and intimately handle a woman. Some women actually allow themselves to suffer through this because he is a "Godly man." He may be able to get by on low sexual skills in some cases, but not knowing how to pleasure a woman decreases his ability to keep a woman happy in that area. Whether it's right or wrong, sex can be a huge factor in good men being single, not to mention bad men having women they don't deserve. A Godly man's mind-set will not focus entirely on sex, but rather how strong is a woman's intimacy toward God. Courtship doesn't require the vain entitlement of a boyfriend or girlfriend, and it doesn't come with fornication. That's our lustful flesh.

Sexual Allurement

Trust me. I Understand sometimes the "spirit is willing but the flesh is weak"... but you must be strong enough to walk away from something your body wants, but your mind knows is not right. Anytime a man says he just wants to have sex, and whatever excuse he gives about not wanting to be in relationships, or whether he calls it "friends with benefits," he is telling you that, to see if you would be okay with it. Also, to let you know that regardless of how much sex you give him, you are not a potential keeper. He probably has a woman already, or he has a friend with benefits. Maybe, he is doing all the real relationship-type stuff with someone else and getting the sex from you, because you showed him you would give it up and not require anything of him in return. Do not allow your mind-set in a relationship to be focused on sex.

Always remember a man can have a sexual relationship with a woman for three years and still not consider her his woman. You need to learn and understand how men think. Even though he had sex with you, once he saw that you were okay with just being a "cut buddy" (sex partner), he knew in his mind that he would never make you more than that. Some men think, "If she will be my cut buddy, or friend with benefits, then how many others of this type of relationship does she have?" He might like you, think you're really cute, like your sex, and even enjoy your company, but still not look at you as the type of woman he is seeking.

Announcement! There is no benefit in this type of relationship for you, and this is definitely not the man that God has destined for your life. If a man even proposes this type of relationship agreement, *run!* (See 1 Corinthians 6:18.)

You can find someone who cares about you and wants to be with you who will not make sex a priority. I have found very, very few, women who could separate their feelings from sex, unless there was money involved. Most of the time when a woman has sex with a man, it changes the dynamics of the relationship for the woman. Typically, she believes that good sex will make him want her and that having a baby will force him to commit to the relationship and be with her. This is far from the truth; these ideas only create room for more hurt. God warns us for a reason that we should abstain and flee from having a sexual relationship until the proper time; because we give away a part of ourselves we can't get back.

Ninety-Day Rule before Sex

The ninety-day rule before having sex, cannot guarantee you anything, but it does increase your chances of weeding some people out. You must be able to filter out the gamer. I don't recommend the ninety-day rule because anyone that's not willing to commit is a waste of time. Period. Being prayerful and using your gift of discernment can help prevent you from wasting too much time. When you value your time, you become wise about how you spend it and who it's spent with. It's always easier for someone else to waste your time when you're already good at wasting it. You usually will know if a relationship is for you in two or three dates-if God has not given you some form of confirmation-move on. Many people will tell you that men love a challenge, but I beg to differ. Godly men don't like a challenge, they like someone who is real, honest, has standards, and sticks to them. Most women put up a wall, believing that playing hard to get is proving something. Playing these types of games can be one reason why some women are single. The truth is, you shouldn't play hard to get, but play hard to sleep with, if anything. Granted, there are always exceptions to every rule, but that's not often. Regardless of what you have heard or may have read in other books, a Godly man who has been truly delivered and is connected to God does not make sex his priority. It's not that you are unattractive or that he prefers the same gender sex; but when he is unsure if someone is connected to his purpose or not on course with God's destiny for his life, he tends to fall back. It's the Samson-and-Delilah

Chapter 5

effect; he understands that sex can be a weakness, so he will try to approach it as God intended it to be.

Appreciate when he tells you that he is not ready for sex. What he is really saying is that God is working on him; then his decisions will make more sense to you later. Please appreciate that! If you insist or try to use your body to make suggestive comments to persuade him otherwise, he may even indulge in the temptation, but in his mind, he has already come to the conclusion that you are not wife material. You both are wrong at this point, and this behavior has jeopardized your relationship.

I can't say I totally agree with this rule, because if we were to be honest, we should not have a ninety-day rule; we should not engage in sexual activities until we are married. I don't believe God is just trying to prevent us from enjoying something as fulfilling as sex. He just wants us to realize the sacredness of sex and doesn't want us to treat it like any other recreational activity. Sex before marriage — that is, premarital experiences, assuming one is talking of sexual intercourse or perversion of the same — and the Word of God imply it all by calling it fornication. It knows no exception. It allows none. Renaming fornication does not change the act or remove the consequence of those who commit fornication sin. It is not in your best interest to have sex with anyone during the time of acclimation of dating.

That's if you are looking for a lasting relationship that will not only be fulfilling but also set a moral standard. Can a relationship cultivate and end up in marriage after sex during this period? Yes, but the chances are not probable. Ninety percent of the Godly men that I interviewed stated, "if a woman wanted to sleep with them within ninety days, they would not consider them to be the person they would like to marry. Godly men sometimes lose interest quickly in women who are easy. Even though there are some men who say they don't really care how soon you sleep with them, usually it's because they have no intention of making you their main chick. Their goal is to add you to their list of sex relationships, so they will play along and pretend that it's not an issue. But at the same time, you will be labeled as a freak, and the average man will have sex with you; and excuse my expression, but you become recreational sex.

Some of these relationships do progress into marriages, kids, etc., but you have to be careful that it's not based solely on sex. If it is based solely on sex, there will come a day when the sex gets boring or less active, they will begin to engage with someone outside of the relationship to fulfill their desires. I don't agree with set, determined times or games because God ultimately should be leading and guiding you (Prov. 3:5–6). If you are being led by God that means you will be praying and utilizing your discernment when it comes to sex.

Sexual Attachments

You can't sow lust and expect to reap love…

You have to remember that you are trying to fulfill your Godly destiny, and you can't attach yourself to anybody simply because of the sex. You can't build a relationship on lust, and try to convince yourself that it's love. Time will tell. So take the time to evaluate if this person is God sent or not, mainly through prayer, and allow God to confirm if the connection exists (not sexual chemistry). If you are truly looking for something serious, then this segment of this book is relevant. If you know you want more, it's in your best interest to hold off on sex, hopefully until marriage. Premarital sex, even in

Chapter 5

the effort to reach compatibility, is not an innocent game to play, according to the Word. God says it is fornication, sin, and those who commit such things shall not inherit the kingdom of God. It is not sex that God condemns, but its misuse outside the marriage bond (1 Cor. 6:18). Sex is not a requirement for love and getting to know someone. Love does not come from kissing, caressing and having sex.

Sex causes emotional and lustful thoughts which lead you to judging things from a lustful and emotional perspective; that's how you feed lust... If you expect to meet people with pure motives to love and be committed to you, sex should not be a casual event. Close the gate, and Let the player play games on someone else's field. You know the relationship is moving too fast when you know more about their genitals, than their goals and dreams.

Control the environment. Your body should never be the main focal point!

Let me share an example. Before I was married, I visited a famous fast-food chicken restaurant drive-through, and I began to place my order. The young lady caught my eye and came back to the drive-through window and bent down to my car while exposing a large amount of cleavage and said, "We don't have any more dark meat. I'm going to have to give you a breast." She tried to lure me with her revealing clothing of her breast.

A man who looks for a one-night stand may love that, but not the man seeking a wife. The kind of guy you will attract or will receive attention from sometimes can be determined by the clothing you wear. I know what men want. Trust me, I am a man. I know more men than you do, and I know them better. I know what we think, what we talk about, what we want, and what we look for, and it is different for each one of us, depending on our relationship with God.

I'm sure you already know this, but men were created different from you. We have different desires and priorities. Our eyes and minds react very differently to some things than yours. It isn't disgusting, perverted, or wrong. It's wonderful and good! It is how God made us. But it's how we handle these differences that separate a Godly man from a worldly man. A worldly man doesn't try to control himself; rather, he looks at anything that attracts his attention and will sleep with anyone who gets him excited.

What You Advertise, Is What You Attract

"Confidence" supersedes any type of make up a woman can wear to appear more beautiful.

Are you dressing to be respected or to be seen? That should always be the question when you're in your closet. *Men will not consider a woman "wife material" that dresses for the attention, and goes where she knows she'll get a lot of it.* Ladies, there has to be more to your life than you dressing up, going out, and hoping a man notices you in your see thru dress. How else do you plan to enjoy your life?

If all you aim to show is body parts, you're going to attract men who want you for your body parts. You can have a career, a degree, a great body, 36 inch weave, mac cosmetics, red bottoms, and still be worthless to a man... who has lost respect for you. When you start trying to please and appeal to God, everything begins to change – speech, dress, habits, thoughts, and life. The difference between a woman who's about respect- and a woman, who's about attention, shows in their attire, speech, and actions. The real beauty is in not

Chapter 5

wanting or needing any validation based on what you look like. If you want to attract the right man and relationship, put less focus on being attractive and more focus on your inner beauty or spirit. Mr. Wrong has no problem when girls wear clothes that show off skin, like boxers, high- or low-cut shirts, low-rise jeans, and cute little swimsuits. He's a fan of revealing shirts and pants that show off everything; he thinks they're fine! The worldly man who watches a lot of TV and R-rated movies isn't really offended by sexual content or nudity and usually secretly dabbles in pornography. This man claims to be a Christian and makes up a significant portion of your church and youth group. He's a really nice guy but sees you mainly for your body. If you were to marry a worldly guy, he'd bring lots of baggage into the relationship, have intimacy problems, entertain thoughts of other women, and possibly cheat on you. A Godly man prays to control his drive and desires. He constantly seeks God and reads and lives the Word of God. He walks in the Spirit and isn't set off by everything he sees in the flesh.

When immodestly dressed girls, magazine covers, or risqué advertisements come into view, a Godly man quickly "bounces his eyes" away from the image. He's constantly guarding his thoughts and what he allows into his mind. He hates being around girls who disrespect themselves, him and his struggles by wearing inappropriate attire. A Godly man will view you as a person, honor you and respect you as a woman. He has your best interests in mind and guards against inappropriate thoughts of you. If you were to marry a Godly man, he would give you the emotional attention you need. He would ignore other women and remain faithful to you no matter what, when God is head of his life.

Unfortunately, there are more worldly men than Godly men, and to make matters worse, to the untrained eye, a worldly man can look a lot like a Godly man.

So what can you do to attract only Godly men?

An important way of delineating between the two of them lies in how you dress. Selling the wrong image of you will get you all the wrong buyers. As mentioned before, the clothes you wear advertise what kind of man you are looking for. If you dress immodestly, you will attract worldly men and push away the Godly ones. It all comes down to the kind of man you want to spend your time around and eventually marry. You cannot afford to be complacent in this area of your life! You will pay the price someday.

This issue isn't limited strictly to you and your future relationship. The way you dress directly affects other men and women and their relationships. You don't see the struggles, the pain, the tears, and the sin that you cause, but I can promise that you would be shocked if you did! Ask any Christian young man; we've all seen it. It's kept hidden, but it is definitely there. By dressing immodestly, you effectually spit on the struggles of our weaker ranks, appearing to care more about toying with us than helping us. You'll never know how many broken relationships and lifestyles of sin you've contributed to simply by the way you dress. I'm not saying it's all your fault, because the lust has to first be in a man's heart before it can bring forth sin (James 1:15). So the man has the primary responsibility to deal with his issues.

Of course, I understand the desire to look stylish, attractive, and cute. It's important to fit in and get attention. Trust me, it can be done modestly! I also understand that it is

Chapter 5

easier for some girls to find stylish and well-fitting clothes than it is for others. This is an area where men really don't understand what you are up against.

But just remember, for every sacrifice you make to honor God with your image and body, Godly men are making sacrifices in their lives that are just as hard, if not harder. They will and do respect you so much for choosing to be modest. A real lady is conscientious of the image she presents, and real men want a real lady. You can forget about any guys missing out on how attractive you are, because you don't wear revealing clothing to appear sexy. To attract the Godly man, you could wear a bedspread or sweat pants, and he would still know you're sexy because he's attracted to the inner beauty (1 Pet. 3:4); and understands that true beauty is watered by confidence. It's time to end sex as a recreational sport. It's past time for Godly men and Virtuous women to commit to each other-raise the standard and walk with God. Having values, dignity and knowing your value, are true signs of maturity, because at some point you will be tested on the validity of your self-worth; and If you don't expect the best.....you will never get it!!

Chapter 6

When Love Hurts: Overcoming Bad Relationships, Abuse, Hurt, and Divorce

So the relationship didn't work out for some reason and you have broken up with who you thought was your soul mate, your confidant and best friend. Now what? First and foremost, decide with your heart, soul, and spirit if you really love this person. No amount of time will matter if the love you have for this person is real. The time since the break-up could be a week, a month, a year, five years, or more before you are back together, but if you love him/her then it doesn't matter. But, don't put your life on hold. Every minute you spend focusing on your ex is a minute that's holding you back from a better future relationship

True Love

True love is logical, and it's not emotional. It's not a feeling; it's a choice.

If there was a true love connection, which again only you know, then that experience will always rise above any conflict that rears its ugly head in your relationship. In the words of Rod Tidwell from the movie *Jerry Maguire*, "You

Chapter 6

know when you know!" And as mentioned before, only you know that.

Second, you should also know if this person truly loves you. Sometimes it is best to cut your losses, but of course, only you truly know the answer to this question. Even if your ex-partner is seeing someone else and it looks like their relationship is getting closer, do not be discouraged. It is time to woman up and accept this situation. More than likely, this new woman is a rebound for him. If you trust in your heart and soul that your ex has feelings for you based on the relationship you shared, then he does — really! You have to trust that the love that you gave him will prevail during this separation. However, this is not the time to try to woo him with sex or a pregnancy, having a baby will not make him stay-it will only complicate the break-up.

Lastly, give him as much time and space as needed to miss you, and believe me, he will if the memories you shared made him deliriously happy. You might ask, "Well, how long is that?" As long as it takes. Remember, you are in this situation for the long haul, if in fact you love this person. You can never put a time limit on love. If it has been a month since you've contacted your ex, then do so. If an apology is in order, then make it promptly and in person if possible.

You do not need to go overboard, but you do need to be sincere. A mailed letter is required. Let me repeat a mailed letter is required — no phone call, no text message, and no e-mail. If you do not get a response, don't panic. Lack of response could be a good thing. At least he is not telling you to get lost, not to correspond with him, or that it's over.

The following month, write him again and every month thereafter until he responds — and he will. Eventually he will respond either negatively or positively. Either way, you will get the answer you seek. I personally believe that no response is a positive; remember, you are starting from square one again, and it will take some time to rebuild the love you both shared as well as the trust required to move forward. I am a firm believer in fighting for love. It is the foundation of humanity and a cause that is worth attaining. Having said that, please know that it is over once the other person decides to establish a relationship or marry someone else. You *must* let it go!

Let It Go!

God has someone better for you- than the person who is bringing out the worst in you.

When your relationship is going well, you don't have to tell anyone; haters watch, your Ex will notice. You know how some of women do; get a new boo and start throwing parties in your ex's front yard to celebrate. Using your new mate as show and tell, for your Ex is showing your new mate disrespect and telling your Ex "I'm not over you." Who your Ex is dating is none of your business, and how good or bad they look-is absolutely irrelevant. *Sometimes letting go isn't as easy as just dropping trash in a trash can. Pray for peace, pray for help.* Make sure you're not fighting to hold onto someone God is trying to help you let go of. Take your focus off of trying to make your ex feel bad for letting you go, and focus on actually LETTING GO !

When you refuse to let go of the past, you refuse to let yourself live. The memories will choke the faith, joy, love, and life out of you. Recently I had a talk with a thirty-year-old young lady, and I asked her, "What's wrong?" She said, "At the moment, my boyfriend and I are no longer together, and

Chapter 6

I am lying here in my bed remorseful and sad. No matter how hard I try to stay away from him, I just get so sad and frustrated, and then I text him. He's now dating some high school girl he cheated on me with last year. I don't know how I can be so stupid! "After three years of tolerating his lying, cheating, and using me, I still don't get enough. I feel so ugly inside. I feel suicidal, and I just want to die. Although I will not bring myself to do that to me, I don't understand why this has to happen to me. We obviously will not get married or be together forever. It's just not going to happen, regardless of whether we get back together, which we probably will because I'm just that stupid. I know this is not the man for me because he will never change, but I just can't let go."

Shut the Front Door!

Getting over things isn't always as easy as changing the channel on a TV with a remote. It takes prayer.

But you must "Move on. When you forgive, you cut off their power. When you don't, that person has access to a light switch on your emotions. There's no point of living in the past. Just because it's hard, doesn't mean it's impossible." Sometimes pain and hurt can open your eyes from the blindness. Letting go doesn't mean that you don't care about someone anymore. It's just realizing that the only person you really have control over is yourself. I know it's hard sometimes after a bad relationship or a messy divorce to let go. It hurts so bad — I get that — but you must take baby steps towards letting this man go. Every woman has that one man she goes back to, heartbreak after heartbreak and nobody knows why, not even her and she just can't let go. Sometimes the best way to be happy is to learn to let go of people and things you tried so hard to hold on to...It's not what you want to hear, but what other option do you have? You have tried everything from throwing yourself *at* him to forcing yourself *on* him, and he *still* shuts you down. There's nothing else you can do at this point but distance your-self from him and give him his space. Never lose yourself in attempt to hold on to someone who doesn't care about losing you. You must be strong enough to let go and patient enough to wait for God to send you the love that you deserve. You don't need any part time people in your life. They are either with you or they're not, they can't just come and go as they please. If he does loves you the way he said he once did, he will come back. The only thing is, by then you will have moved on.

Don't Be Predictable

Don't be afraid to be different. Fitting in is too common for what God has placed within you. Never present yourself as too available, predictable, clingy, and needy. Men run from those character traits. Make him wonder where you went and what happened to you. That's when you will get your phone call from him. Give him his space, and you will see his true colors. (No phone calls, texts, Facebook messages—*nothing*! No communication at all!) You have to cut your losses and move on. It will be extremely hard to let go; you may love this man dearly and may have invested lots of time and effort in this, but I don't know what good will come out of you loving a man who's not loving you back. There's no way you can force him to love and want you. He has shown and told you he no longer wants you. He has turned rude and disrespectful when you have done nothing wrong to him. For three years, this young lady had dated this man, and in a matter of three weeks, he single-handedly destroyed that bond by exposing the person he really was. This is not the type of man God places in your path. Some are sent to you as a distraction or as a decoy in place of the Godly man that awaits you.

Chapter 6

Know Your Value

I told her, "You have to realize you deserve better than this. He clearly doesn't want to continue the bond you two shared. Although this hurts, for I know you still care for him deeply, you've got to let him go." In your relationship, you must Give, but don't allow yourself to be used ... Love, but don't allow your heart to be abused ... Trust, but don't be naive...When a man wants to walk out of your life, let him. For your sake, it's probably better that you let someone who wants out of your life to leave and allow God to allow the person who wants to be there to walk in. What good will they contribute to your life if they don't even want to respect you? Men, cherish what they respect, whether it's a car, house, money or church. So if he cherishes you, he will respect you.

Ladies, if you don't know your value, neither will He.

You must push yourself to the point where you realize your value as a virtuous woman and do not call him anymore, do not contact him, do not look him up, and do not talk to his family anymore (don't be rude, but inform them of the reason why). Sever all ties. He has shown you his true colors; there is nothing left for you to know about this man. This man is going to expect you to chase after him now that he has basically left you in the dust. Don't live up to his expectations, and don't contact him in any way. "You must make a decision that you are going to move on. It won't happen automatically. You will have to rise up and say, 'I don't care how hard this is, I don't care how disappointed I am, I'm not going to let this get the best of me. I'm moving on with my life and shall overcome this in Jesus name (Phil 4:13)."

Then allow God to heal your hurt before trying to invest in another relationship.

Overcoming The Pain of a Bad relationship

Sometimes the end of a relationship can be traumatic. Moving on is a process, the more you try to rush it the longer the process becomes. You must realize- love didn't hurt you, someone who didn't know how to love, hurt you. Don't confuse the two. You'll lose hope in love. You must forget the past, it's gone, not worth it, and you can't do anything to change it. Focus on the future. Plan what you want, and aim for it. The saddest part of loving someone is when it's not your choice, but you need to let go and say goodbye.

In addition to the loss of the relationship, you may have to contend with changes in your social life, find a new place to live, adjust to living alone, take care of practical arrangements and finances, contend with custody issues if there are children involved, deal with feelings of rejection and abandonment, deal with feelings of inadequacy, betrayal and jealousy if there was another person involved, and somehow find a way to cope with day to day living. If the relationship was abusive or toxic in any way there will be many more feelings to contend with.

In any loss, whether it is a loved one, car, or house, a person typically goes through seven stages of pain. They may not occur in the following order, and some of the stages may coincide with each other. There is no right or wrong way to deal with this pain; no two relationships are the same and every person is different. Even if you initiated the break up, you will still feel a sense of pain and loss.

The issues that occurred in previous relationships may be revisited, and the feelings relived once more. This is more likely to happen if these issues were unresolved and the person has repeated these patterns in subsequent

Chapter 6

relationships. Therapy can be a great source of help in these cases. Talk to your spiritual leader, and sometimes professional help is needed.

The Stages of Pain

When you have truly given your all in a relationship and the person seemed to have walked all over you, when it's over you may experience -Denial. To overcome this you must you must realize that the Pain is the thing that gives you the strength to get better, then you must come to the realization that the relationship is over, but you may want to continue to pursue your ex-partner. Like I said before, you must release them, or it can cause psychosomatic stress that may lead to your body becoming ill. You may experience shock and disbelief. You may not be able to comprehend that the relationship has really ended, and these feelings may be all-consuming. This stage may overlap with the next stage.

Anger comes next. You may seek to blame your ex-partner for the breakup, ruminating on their faults and feeling and expressing a great deal of annoyance and hostility towards them.

There could be some *bargaining*. Bargaining is when you seek to win your ex back, promising to change or make compromises. This stage can be detrimental because it's when you usually lower your standards and do things like trying to trap him by getting pregnant. *Remember, having his baby will NOT bring him back-it may push him further away.*

Then there is *self-blame*. You may begin to accuse yourself for the relationship failure. You must understand that every relationship has its purpose. People come into your life for a reason, a season, or a lifetime and lastly to expose who they really are, so you are able to know their intentions and decide if you need to let them go and move on. At this time, you may have a very low sense of self-esteem. You may wish you had done things differently or said things differently and take on board all of the blame.

Low self-esteem and *depression* may create feelings of sadness or hopelessness, causing you to withdraw from social relationships and spend a lot of time brooding and ruminating. You may cling to memories of your partner, play the same songs repeatedly, and daydream about what might have been.

Lastly, there's *acceptance*. You now begin to feel a fresh sense of hope, and you think of your partner less often. You do not feel the same sense of raw pain and resume social relationships. You may even begin to seek out a new partner. From time to time, you may feel nostalgic, but you will accept that the relationship is now over.

If you are getting over a breakup, it is best to take things slowly, a step at a time. Accept that you will go through these stages and that they won't be easy. Talking things through with a friend or a therapist can help enormously and help you to make sense of the emotions that you're going through.

This is especially important if the relationship was messy in any way. You've finally said you are tired of the manipulation. After time and many promises, you realize nothing has really changed, and you realize it isn't likely to. Recognizing you will never be the captain of your own ship until you take your life back can be difficult, but you *can* do it.

Remember not to beat yourself up or consider yourself foolish. In recognizing your partner as controlling and manipulative, you must also recognize this: though they can at first be charming, controlling and manipulative people are the unfortunate product of an incisive intellect and low self-esteem. They are usually people who, at first blush, seem to be confident, charming, and together. It's no wonder you found your ex-partner attractive.

How to break-up with an Abusive Person

Get to the point, and don't try to cushion the blow or beat around the bush. Your first instinct is to sever the relationship in person (not always advisable, but the honorable first choice) and to hurt your partner as little as possible, but this may only result in prolonging his agony and yours. Come right out and declare your decision frankly, without hostility and being cruel. He will likely be stunned and shocked and may question, attempt to bargain, cry, or become enraged; all are possible reactions. Be prepared for anything.

Make arrangements for a family member, friend or law-enforcement officer to be present if you have any reason to believe he may become violent or if he has access to guns or other weapons. Depending on your situation, your leaving may be best explained in a note. Be clear about your decision, and then leave at once. Example: "I'm so sorry, but this is not working for me anymore, so I'm ending our relationship here. I will always care about you and wish you well, but it's over." Do *not* say, "I will always love you" and then sign it with "XXOO [whoever]"; and do not say, "I'll be at my mom's," or "If you need anything, let me know."

Even if you really do feel this way, this can become the tiny bit of hope your ex-partner needs to continue the obsession with winning you back. If you feel you *must* do this face-to-face, be brief and as dispassionate as possible. (And it's wise to have your things packed and in your car already so that you just need to walk out.) Example: Say, "I just wanted to say this in person. I'm leaving. Our relationship has not worked out for me. I wish you well, but I can't continue this." Then walk out. Don't look back, despite the fact that the person is freaking out, shrieking that you can't go, hanging onto your pant leg, throwing various objects at you, threatening suicide, and generally having a complete meltdown.

The less personal you can bring yourself to be, the better. It seems cold when your inclination is not to want to hurt your former love, but in reality, the less emotional *you* are, the less you will escalate the pain. Believe it. Your ex wants to control you and everything you do, and the more he realizes that he is no longer able to control you, the more intense and hysterical he is likely to become.

It's an effort to engage your feelings of guilt for hurting him, to gain compassion for his pain, etc., as he will take no responsibility for the breakdown of the relationship. He will want to get you to respond as any polite or compassionate person wants to, but once you show any sort of mercy or positive response to this, he knows his rant has worked, and leaving becomes more difficult for you.

Be decisive, and don't fall for promises to change.

Once you have identified your relationship as toxic to your individuality and future, you must take decisive steps. Wishy-washy, weak attempts to leave will be steamrolled, and you will be overrun by the will of your partner. Talking things over with your partner will not be likely to help. Remember the crucial identifier: this is a *controlling manipulator*. As soon as you start making noise about being unhappy with controlling behavior and preparing him for the fact that you are thinking of ending the relationship, he will gladly give in to your desires — just long enough to keep you attached.

He will string you along with little bits of what you need or want to make you believe that he has finally heard you, understands your needs, and is willing to change. The problem is that he is probably not really capable of changing at this point (as evidenced by no change despite many so-called efforts over and over again). As soon as you settle back into the relationship, he knows you're back on the hook, and the bad behavior resumes. It's all just been a kind of ploy to keep you around, continuing a vicious cycle and allowing him to reestablish control.

Leave at Once

Having made your decision, do not waste time. Notice, this is not the first time the exhortation to leave has been made. That's because it's so *hard* to leave, particularly if you decided a face-to-face farewell was necessary. Please believe that your attempts to leave on good terms will most likely not pan out. The truth is, these efforts will only make it *less* likely that you will ever be able to have even the most casual of contact with your ex without it turning into a terrible, embarrassing scene. Your caring response instills hope that control can be reestablished and so feeds the obsession with getting you back, so much so that your partner may abandon all dignity and beg, cry, bargain, scream, etc.

If you leave *before* your ex has completely humiliated himself, it really will end better. No matter how hard it is, turn your back on him, ignoring the begging, sobbing, threatening, and yelling, and put some steel in your back. Walk out the door. Shut it behind you.

Stay Away

Don't be fooled by them saying "I miss you." Sometimes I miss you really means: I want to sleep with you again, I saw that new picture you posted, or you look good I see you happy with someone else. Don't accept phone calls or answer e-mails, instant messages, or text messages from him. Doing so will only create hope. It's likely to end in an unholy debacle, and things will be worse than ever. You won't just have an angry, upset ex; you'll likely end up with a shrieking maniac, freaking out and screeching for your blood. Remember again, this is a controlling, manipulative person who will say anything to *win,* and that is all this contact will be about. Once you have broken away, *stay* away. Having dinner alone with him, "just to talk" or "for the kids' sake" will destroy your resolve and will also give your controlling ex the power he seeks again. Cut it clean, and *let it go.*

For some time after the breakup, avoid mutual friends who are still in contact with your ex. The last thing you need is the passing, even if inadvertent, of more fuel into the fire in the weeks and months after the end of the affair. If you can't avoid contact with these friends, keep your remarks to them carefully neutral, and don't share details of the breakup, your feelings, or your insights on your ex with them. You can almost be assured these remarks will find their way back to your ex, and that will not be a good thing.

Remain Detached

Sometimes you have to stop trying to give them you, and give them space.

In order to reassert control, your ex will look for signs that you are receptive to crying, begging, threats of self-harm, etc.

Chapter 6

If you simply do not react, you will give no fuel to your ex's belief that he can win you back, and it will be truly over much sooner. He will cry, rage, rant, and become hysterical, if *you allow him to*. Being compassionate and trying to comfort or spare your ex further pain will only make it more difficult to break away. Every minute that you stay, talk, commiserate, apologize, or otherwise play along is a *win* for your ex because he knows you feel helpless to leave him in such an awful state.

Remember that there is nothing wrong with you and that what you're going through is normal. You have every right to be happy again, and if you remember that true happiness comes from within and is not dependent upon any one person, you have every chance of finding it. Treat yourself with love and kindness, be gentle with yourself, and try to find one thing in every day that pleases you. Begin by praying each day for thirty minutes and increasing as time goes on.

As I mentioned earlier, these stages can happen in any order, and some people may go through more than one stage at a time, or they may revisit a stage. It's likely that the calm feeling you're describing could be denial or the numb feeling that people often feel initially after a relationship breakdown. Acceptance is the final stage, and it may take time for you to get to this stage, or you may feel it earlier. This often happens as a kind of safety mechanism that enables a person to function immediately after the split.

The calmness acts as a cushion to protect you in the immediate stages. Often it's only after you have dealt with the immediate issues that reality sets in. There is no right way or wrong way to grieve, as everyone is different. Some people may skip stages. Time is the only remedy that works. As time passes, the pain will also pass.

It may take a month, six months, a year, or longer (usually around three months for me, if it was a real relationship), but one morning you'll wake up and realize that God has given you the power to overcome (Rom. 8:37).

These feelings that you experience are quite normal. It's very important that you are kind to yourself at this time and treat yourself with compassion. What seems to be enormous now will gradually lessen, and in time you will feel like yourself again. If the feelings become unbearable, please seek help from a doctor, a therapist, or your spiritual leader.

In addition, learn to *do you*, and focus on moving on and being happy. This isn't going to be easy at first. It's going to be hard; but God's time heals all wounds, and I promise it will get easier with time. Like bad weather, this pain shall pass, and your sunny days will return. Anytime you have any urge to be back with him, forgive him but remember the pain and disrespect he gave you, and turn it into an outlet for finding happiness. God will ensure that the pain you experienced is turned into purpose.

The best revenge on an ex is to be happy loving yourself. Which is a better feeling: being able to say, "He changed for me" or being able to say, "He is the God-sent man for me"? You deceive yourself by thinking you can change a man. You can't. Only a man who is willing to be submitted unto God truly understands the need for change and how to love a woman. Please don't set yourself up for failure, thinking otherwise.

You Had To Date Them

A woman has every right to be extra cautious about a man who doesn't have a plan.

Chapter 6

Most women will spend most of their lives waiting on a man to get his act together.

Through the ups and downs, good and bad, they remain patient. Even if the bad times outweigh the good, they still find a way to hold on to hope, have faith in the relationship, and believe that everything is going to work out. That's the kind of faith God expects us to have in Him. But that's not always the kind of faith we should have in our relationships. You can literally miss out on Mr. Right, by waiting too long for Mr. Wrong to GET right! According to Ephesians 5:16, time is the currency of the relationship, spend it wisely.

Jeremiah 29:11 says, " 'For I know the plans I have for you,' declares the Lord, 'plans to prosper you and not to harm you, plans to give you hope and a future.' " This means that every one of your relationships that didn't work out was for your good. God has someone better for you. Once you start to adopt this way of thinking, there's no need to stress or wonder if you're going to make it through the storm. God's plans will always prevail. We only need to trust Him with all our heart and pray. Continued prayer is continued power!

Chapter 7

Enhancing Your Marriage

By wisdom a house is built, and by understanding it is established; and by knowledge the rooms are filled with rare and beautiful treasures.
— PROVERBS 24:3–4

Laughter is an essential part of marriage.

Having trouble in your relationship/marriage? You're not alone. Even the happiest marriages go thru tough times. Every marriage has a weak moment; don't allow those moments to define your marriage

When I met my wife Tammy, it wasn't just her pretty smile, sexy body or even the Godly spirit that she possessed; it was her sense of humor that drew me to her. Many women in my past were beautiful, smart, creative but lacked personality. I believe what has kept us together through thick and thin is our ability to laugh together. Often! Sometimes too often, we don't get any work done. You must find ways to make you marriage enjoyable; and it can't be based on conditions like money, sex, or materialistic stuff. It's when being together in each other's presence-and finding humor in almost every situation. Every morning we wake up early enough to have a cup of coffee, hug and a smile together showing gratefulness that we are glad to see each other. Oftentimes, when we laugh together, it feels like we are falling in love over and over, and over again. Many times we were faced with hurtful situation; although it did hurt, we realize in order to create a healthy solution to the problem, we had to look past the pain and enjoy the laughter of the brighter moments.

Finally, brethren, whatsoever things are true, whatsoever things are honest, whatsoever things are just, whatsoever things are pure, whatsoever things are lovely, whatsoever things are of good report; if there be any virtue, and if there be any praise, think on these things.
-Phil 4:8(kjv)

Godly Friends

You have a right not to associate with anyone who will influence your relationship to go in the wrong direction.

Choose your associations wisely. One of the most profound lessons that I learned in our marriage: was to use discernment when selecting friends. I trusted too many people with my relationship secrets: later learned that I must be careful with who you choose to trust. Remember your best friend possibly has another best friend, who has a best friend...the list goes on. Try to surround yourself with married couples who will hold you accountable for your actions. No business can sustain itself without prayer, and the help and trust of a good partner of some sort, whether it is a supplier, wholesaler, or just a copartner working in unity. Likewise, in a marriage you must have people around you that you can trust for advice when times get rocky, as they so often do. Sometimes in order to change your marriage destination, you have to change your associations. Being connected to such people can be edifying, fulfilling, and give you a sense of balance, and it seems to keep things in perspective when you run into relationship issues. People with strong marriages can enhance your marriage just by your being around the couple.

I remember one time, Tammy and I got into an argument just prior to attending a cookout at another pastor's house. On the way there, we didn't say a word to each other. All I could think about was how I was going to fix this before we arrived at our friend's house without their knowing what was really going on. When we arrived, our friends were so exuberant with love and happiness as we all began to talk, that Lady Tammy and I forgot we had just been arguing in the car. We soon began to talk about old times, laughing and enjoying the presence of each other.

It wasn't just about the good time we had, but somehow the joy of the Lord that they had on them overflowed onto us. And many times the same thing has happened when our friends came around us. So many times we have invited a couple to dinner or an event who were having relationship issues, and they left totally resolved. But these kinds of friends will not just show up by chance; you must pray and be intentional when meeting people. Ask yourself, "Is this friendship a good or bad influence on my marriage?" If the relationship is good, you must continue to pray for the relationship, and if it's not, pray that God will remove it.

A couple who really has the fear of God in them isn't going to mesh well with someone who doesn't, because their lifestyles aren't going to the same.

You may wonder why I am writing this segment first in the marriage chapter. It's mainly because your more influential relationships must be people who know God and love the Lord, or you will eventually run into unnecessary trouble. Proverbs 12:26 states the wicked or ungodly friend can and will lead you astray. So the first step in enhancing your marriage is to find a church home, that exudes that same type of love and joy that you wish to see in your marriage.

Once your mate has found some godly friends, please allow them to fellowship and bond without you feeling insecure. According to Proverbs 27:17, these friends should make your mate better, and likewise, your mate should sharpen their character also. Here are some areas to focus on while trying to enhance your marriage:

Communicate, Communicate, Communicate...

There are many communication barriers that you have to contend with in relationships in today's society, like social networks or a busy schedule; which can cause you to not be sociable towards your partner. You must ensure that the both of you learn and find time to communicate, even when you disagree. Don't avoid each other and push things to the side. Talk it out like grown folks. Assuming will have you thinking that the relationship is going down the right road, when it's really heading down the wrong one. Don't leave your spouse guessing on how to make the marriage/relationship better. Fully communicate your feelings, needs and boundaries to each other. A lot of the happiness in your Marriage depends on the quality of your communication. Just remember that the first step in this process is-someone must agree to listen because communication is a two-way street. During your attempts to communicate, don't lie to your partner-just to keep them happy. Honesty is a necessity in any relationship. You must discuss any major decisions with each other, don't hide money in secret bank accounts, lie about your days off work or buy a car or major purchase just because you have the larger income in the relationship. If you don't gather your partner's opinion before making a decision that impacts you both, you're just starting trouble for now or later; and don't be afraid to allocate roles and duties in the home in a way that works for your family

Minister in Your Home First

Many times we neglect the people who are most important to you simply because you think they will always be there. God has blessed us with our mate, even-though we love them-we find ourselves getting complacent with their presence. Don't stop being lovey dovey and mushy to each other. That's not an "in the beginning thing" it's a love thing. We have to be careful not to get blessed with a great mate and then begin to take them for granted or get complacent. You cannot get so busy with your job, pastoring, ministering to other family, friends, coworkers, that you neglect your spouse and forget to nurture your own family and/or marriage. It's okay to say "no" to other people demand of your time. Stop and listen when your spouse comes to you and wants to talk. Take a break from work, homework, or your hobby; instead of being annoyed by the interruption, be grateful for the moment.

Making time for your relationship/marriage is your greatest and most important investment. When outside endeavors, becomes more important than your relationship; your endeavors will start dictating your solution, and leave your relationship unbalance. When you take your marriage/ relationship for granted, it will invite attention from the outside and it can cause your marriage to dilapidate. When you "sow" your all into your marriage you'll be amazed at what will "grow."

Chapter 7

Insecurities

In order to love your spouse in the way he or she fully deserves, you must first pour energy into healing the root of your insecurities.

Usually your insecurities are caused by some form of hurt or jealousy, whether it's from the past or your present relationship. If jealousy is something you've always carried with you, then you have to look inward to your own history and your own personality for understanding and solutions. Perhaps you don't know why, but you frequently check up on your spouse, without provocation. Your spouse hasn't done anything even suspicious, yet you're checking up.

Maybe you're monitoring your spouse's dress habits: "Aren't you dressed up fancy just to go to work?" Do you fly into a rage if your spouse gets home from work a few minutes late? Do you feel like you have to control the finances just so you can have control over what your spouse can afford to do or where your spouse can go? Do you listen in on your spouse's phone conversations even if there's been no unusual or suspicious behavior? If these describe you, you need to do some introspection and change the way you talk to yourself.

Your internal dialogue should argue against ideas that support your jealous feelings. You might be able to work this out on your own. Or you might not be able to do this on your own by sitting down and discussing the matter with your mate. Or you might need to be in psychotherapy, either individually or as a couple. Even though you might think of this as only an individual issue, it is impacting your relationship/marriage.

Swallow Your Pride

You and your mate must realize that having a submissive wife/husband is NOT about controlling them or thinking you can do and say anything, and they must comply.

Sometimes you have to swallow your pride and accept that you're wrong. Avoid childish confrontations at all costs. Sometimes even proving your point, profits nothing. It's not called giving up; it's called growing up. Pride can cause one or both spouses to think that they are better than the other or entitled to certain benefits simply because of whom they are or what they have done. Pride is a husband who refuses to help out with the housework or the children because he "works hard every day." His assumption in this case is that his wife does not work as hard as he does and that he deserves a break because of all his hard work. Pride is a wife who shares her greatest joys and fears with someone other than her husband because "he never understands me." In reality, pride can prevent us from strengthening our marriage. It can prevent us from healing in our relationship after we have been hurt (or have hurt our spouse). Learn to agree to disagree, and move on. Be understanding towards your partner. Don't expect them to understand your opinion... when you don't want to understand theirs. A simple seven step process usually helps: pray, state problem, validate their view, suggest a solution, mutually agree on the plan, apologize for any wrong, kiss and hug.

Sex as a Weapon

Be sexually generous with your husband/wife (1 Cor. 7:2-4).

Anything frigid in our homes should have food in it! Don't ignore your mate's needs. If it's important to your mate, it's important for your marriage. "The husband must fulfill his [sexual] duty to his wife, and likewise also the wife to her husband. The wife does not have authority over her own body, but the husband does; and likewise also the husband does not have authority over his own body, but the wife does. Stop depriving one another [of sex]" (1 Cor. 7:3–5). Cultivate the marriage bed frequently, and reap the many rewards. Marital sex can uplift, unite, comfort, and console, but it must not be used to manipulate, coerce, dominate, or control. Sex blesses if the marriage is healthy. Sex stresses if the marriage is not. Focus on ordinary daily acts of love, and the sex can be hot!

Be Sexually Creative

When having sex, be creative.

Be open for change. What once worked for your marriage 10 years ago, may not work for your marriage now. Try changing your style a little, what you said you would never wear-may be just what he likes. Try new things during intercourse, take initiative and not be so passive. Inactivity during sex is like having sex with a dead body. Turn the TV off and your spouse on! There is no reason for you and your spouse to be sitting on the couch watching mindless TV. Use this time to ignite some much-deserved fire! You're not just a husband or a wife. You're a lover. Go make some love! If you use to wear sexy lingerie when you were first married, don't replace that with flannel pajamas (unless your mate finds them sexy); I don't care how old you think you are. Don't assume you know everything about your partner's body. Ask where your spouse likes to be touched the most. Make it a habit to always try new positions and places, and start making mad love! If you're going to wear sexy lingerie or pajamas, you must wear it with confidence.

You must work it like you're worth it! Men are aroused by what they see; women are aroused by what they feel. Throw out the rule book, ladies; let him see you with the lights on sometimes. Be confident about your body, and have fun! A marriage that lacks good sex is a marriage that isn't going smooth. The more you love your mate-the more intimate you want to be with them.

Be Patient with Each Other During Hard Times

In every marriage, there will be obstacles.

Strong marriages are not just about the good times you share; they're also about the obstacles you go through together. Disagreements are a natural part of healthy relationships, but it's important that you find a way to compromise if you disagree on something. During hard times you must treat your spouse like you would want to be treated, with love, trust, honesty, courtesy, honor and respect. No mate is perfect, don't expect a mate who doesn't make mistakes, doesn't make you mad at times, annoys you sometimes and so forth; we are all human. You won't always have days where you feel in love with your spouse. Don't let those days to cause you to go astray, fight through the bad emotions. There will be times when your mate may lose a job, become disabled, or just suffer a major setback or obstacle. The conquering of those obstacles and the growing together are the gratifying parts of a relationship. You must remain patient with each other; communicate the problem in prayer, before trying to handle it on your own merit. God can change the things you can't. When you begin to take accountability for yourself, and really understand grace and mercy; it humbles you and makes it easier for you to forgive your mate. Patience is the key; it demonstrates that you understand your mate is human and that you understand we all fall short sometimes.

Chapter 7

When adversity hits you like a ton of bricks, it can easily throw you into a pit of discouragement and despair. When things appear to be falling apart, focus on one thing, take one step at a time. If the problem is financially related, agreeing to make every financial decision together will help to control where your money goes and shouldn't go. Although you may consider hard times and difficulties as a setback, God see them as times for great advancement of the relationship. His purpose for allowing them is not to destroy you, but to stimulate your spiritual growth together in your relationship. In His great wisdom, the Lord knows how to take an awful situation and use it to transform you into the image of Christ and equip you to carry out His will.

Every adversity that comes into your life is sifted through God's permissive will. That doesn't mean the difficulty itself is His perfect will, but He's allowed the trial to touch you, so that He can use it to accomplish His wonderful purposes for your life. Although some of the suffering we see and experience seems senseless or blatantly evil, we must recognize that we have a very limited perspective and cannot always understand what the Lord is doing.

You Hurt My Feelings

Conflict is a normal, healthy way to grow closer to your spouse. Use wisdom in communicating. Many say "I can't get my spouse to open up to me?" Well stop shutting down or blowing up like a bomb, when they tell you the truth...and communicate. Words spoken out of respect and love will be heard and understood more than rude words spoken from rage. Know when to speak, when to listen, how much to say, and how much to hold. Instead of becoming defensive, focus on the issue at hand. Learn to agree to disagree before the peace leaves the conversation. Once the peace is gone, someone's feelings are going to get hurt. So often, pride gets in the way of resolving conflict. We don't like to be wrong, so our pride ends up damaging our relationships. Pride in winning the argument is never worth losing the love. Agree to disagree until there's enough peace for a compromise.

God sees every aspect of life, but our view is restricted to what is right before us. Though we'll never grasp the infinite mind of God, we can know His faithfulness and love. When you can't understand God's ways, focus on His perfect knowledge, wisdom, and power to guide you and your spouse rather than on the magnitude of your emotions or sorrow. Remember, He sees the entire picture and loves you more than you can imagine. This is a time to walk by faith and to pray for understanding of the situation (Prov. 3:5) and how to work through it and move on. Lifelong relationships will never have quick fixes. Be patient with each other's; mistakes, frustrations, trials.... take time to resolve, repair & rebuild. Then, be willing to let go of the things that are out of your control. Take ownership of the things that are. Above all, pray to God for wisdom and discretion.

Love and Listen

Happy marriages are based on a deep friendship. Loving your partner means going out of your way to show him or her acts of love, like you would do for a best friend. If you have had a stressful day, lean on your spouse. Don't suffocate one another by neediness, but know when your spouse needs TLC the most. No matter your mood, no matter your own day, lift your spouse up. Choose to serve your spouse. Knowing what they like, what they love, what they dislike, and what they hate. Attentiveness is necessary. How often we expect more from our spouses than we are willing to give! We can either selfishly demand our way or unselfishly give up our own way

Chapter 7

and bless our spouses in every possible way. It's not hard to see which choice would foster a lasting and joyful marriage.

If your mind wanders to your spouse and you think to yourself, "I love this about you," don't keep it to yourself. Share your sentiments! Why hold back any love for your spouse? Don't make your spouse work for your love. Give it freely and fully! It's important to tell your partner what you love about him or her. Whether they be sentimental words or naughty words, shed some serious love!

Focus daily on being a good listener to your spouse. Listening will show your mate that you care more about him or her than you do about yourself. Inspire your spouse to be a better person. Challenge your mate in all the right areas, and be an ear to listen. Set some rules like not interrupting until the other is through speaking or banning phrases such as "you always" or "you never." It's easy to let personal beliefs and opinions get in the way of earnestly listening to your spouse. Know when your spouse just wants to be heard. There are times when your partner needs to hear that they are doing a good job as a spouse and parent. Reassure them Make a point to share about your day with your spouse. Once you stop sharing, it becomes easy to let communication slip.

Never Stop Dating

When you have days off, get out of the house, and take your mate on a date.

Even when you are married, don't stop thinking of your mate as your boyfriend/girlfriend. Keep dating them and doing your best to continue winning their heart. Get a babysitter, get some loving — whatever it takes! When you and your spouse plunk yourself on the couch for hours on end, ur relationship to fall into a path of stagnancy. ouse need to do active things together; if not, ...onship mirrors that. Get up and get out! Build date nights into your schedule; make it a part of your lifestyle. If you have the day off today, you have a plentiful amount of time to do something nice for your spouse — and to do something a little naughty, too!

A beautiful marriage bed needs many of the same things as a beautiful flower bed- Work!

Among them are caring hands. Be a snuggler, be an ear, be a romancer, be a mirror, be a lover, be a date, be a friend, be a mate, and break the routine. Mix up your relationship habits to keep your marriage fresh. Speaking of opposites, if you always get intimate with the lights off, give it a go with the lights on. If you usually have the TV on at the end of the day, keep it off tonight and have a good conversation. Make tonight about opposites. If your spouse usually cooks dinner, how about you give it a go? Be spontaneous in the relationship. If you don't have kids, try cooking dinner in the nude.

Never Nag

Don't sweat the small stuff.

When you have the urge to nag your spouse about something, give it five minutes and remind yourself that your role is not to nag. You have to be able to rightly divide their nagging from the things you really need to hear. It can all come in the same breath. Not all of their complaining is senseless. Take the time to listen; you may experience less complaining, and gain more understanding about your relationship. When you start focusing on your reasons to be thankful, you will start losing reasons to complain. Nagging a man or woman to change is a form of strangling the relationship. You'll choke the life out of their efforts. Nagging never changes a person — prayer does. You shouldn't complain about what you're not willing to pray about, communicate the problem in prayer before trying to handle it on your own merit. God can change the things you can't. Pray that truth replaces and heals whatever issue you feel the need to nag about. Try holding your mate's hand and asking him or her to pray with you about the issue.

Replace bitterness with forgiveness. You want to be a blessing to your spouse, not a burden. When your spouse is down in the dumps, drop what you're doing and hug him or her. Your touch is soothing to your spouse. Be sure your tendency toward technology doesn't take up time better spent engaging in heart-to-heart communication with your spouse. It's insulting to your mate if you start texting and logging on to Facebook, etc., or calling a friend while your spouse is trying to enjoy communication or a romantic moment.

Value Your Relationship

Don't waste time comparing your marriage to those of your friends, or allow your friends to compete with your marriage.

A real friend will respect your relationship and won't get upset when you tell them: "You need to spend quality time alone with your mate." If they can't understand that, you may need to check your circle to see if they are really for your relationship or not. Also, love your spouse for the person they are, not who your friends want them to be, not who they used to be, not who you want them to be, but who they are today. Comparison is the thief of joy. Insecurity is the biggest turnoff. Embrace who you are, and let loose and have fun! Take a moment to ask yourself if you would care to be married to you. If the answer is no, it's time to make a few changes. Marriage should never be tit for tat. Keeping score in your marriage is a quick way to plant a toxic seed in your relationship. Understanding another person's point of view does not invalidate yours but provides greater perspective, understanding, and empathy.

Learn to give your spouse the benefit of the doubt. Giving your mate the benefit of the doubt means when you do not have all the information, even in conflict, you are willing to assume the best, put negative judgment aside, and respond favorably. You cannot allow negativity to overcome your mind; it will have you internalizing every assumption you can think of. Love gives the benefit of the doubt. It seeks to work through difficult situations, even when you are disappointed or proven wrong. The Bible says love "bears all things, believes all things, hopes all things, and endures all things" (1 Cor. 13:7). This does not mean that love is naïve. It does, however, mean that love gives the benefit of the doubt.

Never Give Up

It's never too late to rekindle the flame in your marriage.

Something women often don't understand: men are not mind readers. If you don't tell him how you feel, he's not going to know. If you are feeling neglected, feel like you are not receiving the attention you deserve, and even feel the urge to cheat, it's time to talk out these issues and start the dating process with your mate all over again to do more and love each other enough to remove these thoughts. If you communicate and work together, a fresh start is totally an option. There's something you must understand: if your spouse makes a point to express love and affection, make sure you make a point to receive it. If you hardly acknowledge your mate all day, they won't want to get intimate with you at night.

Remain a Power Couple.

If you're not willing to pray with you man/woman for God to help you establish a health relationship, you're not ready to have one.

One of the secrets of promoting a healthy relationship between husband and wife is to pray together, respect and support each other's legitimate interests. Pray for your marriage and spouse, no one outside of your marriage will be able to do it better than you. Encourage and celebrate each other's successes, no matter how big or small. Setting unattainable expectations will leave your spouse feeling as if he or she is constantly unable to satisfy you. Try not to major on the negatives and minor on the positives.

Stand strong during the hard times. Never mistake a disconnect from your Spouse with falling out of Love. It means to take a time out to learn what and where each other have changed. Any marriage can last when the sun is shining. In the storms of the relationship is where love is supposed to shine the brightest. In the storms is where you develop the character of the relationship. So try to highlight the good about your spouse. Learn to forgive each other. Forgiveness can lower your blood pressure, strengthen your immune system, and drop the level of the stress hormones. Sometimes you may need to take breaks from each other. Occasional space can create more affection.

Plan Quality Time

You both must intentionally plan for quality time to strengthen your marriage.

Don't make it a habit to be late to come home at night. Many homes disintegrate simply because of *time*. Set a day or several days out of the week to spend time together, regardless of your work schedules, job requirements, school assignments, kids, or family. And do not deviate! Commit to this time, whether it is two hours or ten hours together. Be creative, and be sure to make conversation about the relationship, family status, plans, or interests at this time. That's it!

Then find some time to deepening your prayer life together (1 Thess. 5:17) and deepening your intimacy with each other and God. Learn to appreciate whom you have instead of focusing on whom others have. Above all, be slow to anger and quick to forgive (Luke 17:3–4).

Respect

Never belittle your mate, especially in front of others. Even-though they may get on your last nerve, save the conversation until you can talk about it in private.

Last and not Least-

Now, write down 5 things you promise to work on for your relationship/marriage. Fold in half and write "I promise" on the front of it. Pray over what you wrote, and then give it to your spouse. Now-Go to Work!!!

Chapter 8

Virtuous Women Rock!

By Pastor Tammy Brown

An excellent wife is the crown of her husband, but she who causes shame is like rottenness in his bones.
— Proverbs 12:4

Ladies, Treat your man like bird, hold them too tightly, you suffocate them. Hold them too loosely, they'll fly away. Hold them with love and care, they remain with you forever.

You must allow him to be the man in the relationship. Stop trying to take that position.

A *real man* will lead you to God and not away from Him. He will never be a distraction, but he will always be an asset. Set your standards and don't compromise, when a man truly loves you, he will put you before any other human being. Notice I said "human." God is always first, and I understand that (LK 10:27). A real man would not compliment others and never compliment you. You should never feel that you have to compete with other women or men in his life. They should

91

know that you are his queen. A real man, the kind of man a woman wants to give her life to, is one who will respect her dignity, who will honor the valuable treasure God has instilled in her. A real man will not attempt to rip her precious pearl from its protective shell or persuade her with charm to give away her treasure prematurely, but he will wait patiently until she willingly gives him the prize of her heart. A real man will cherish and care for that prize forever. *I encourage you to cultivate the 22 points about the excellent virtuous woman:* (Proverbs 31: 10–31)

1. Vs-10–SHE IS RARE,
2. Vs-11–SHE IS TRUSTWORTHY,
3. Vs12–SHE IS CONSTANT IN Her LOVE,
4. Vs-13–SHE IS INDUSTRIOUS,
5. Vs-14–SHE IS THRIFTY,
6. Vs15–SHE IS SELF-STARTING,
7. Vs-16–SHE IS ENTERPRISING,
8. Vs- 17–SHE IS WILLING TO DO HARD WORK,
9. Vs-18–SHE IS WILLING TO WORK LONG HOURS,
10. Vs-19– SHE IS WILLING TO DO MONOTONOUS WORK,
11. Vs-20–SHE IS COMPASSIONATE,
12. Vs-21–SHE IS PREPARED FOR THE FUTURE,
13. Vs-22–SHE IS A GOOD SEAMSTRESS,
14. Vs-23–SHE IS MARRIED TO A LEADER, FOR THE UNMARRIED, SHE IS MARRIED TO CHRIST,
15. Vs-24–SHE IS AN ENTREPRENEUR,
16. Vs-25–SHE IS NOT SWAYED BY CIRCUMSTANCES,
17. Vs-26–SHE IS WISE AND KIND,
18. Vs-27–SHE IS DUTY CONSCIOUS,
19. Vs-28–SHE IS BLESSED BY HER FAMILY,
20. Vs-29–SHE IS NOT SATISFIED WITH THE MEDIOCRE,
21. Vs-30–SHE IS A WOMAN OF GOD,
22. Vs-31–AND SHE IS PRAISEWORTHY.

Chapter 8

Never Compromise

Loving the person God has for your life will never require compromising your standards, integrity, faith, or body. When you appear desperate or don't have self-value, you attract people looking to take advantage of you. Believing that you're beautiful inside and out is the first step to understanding your worth as a woman. When you seek a man to fill a void in your life, in the end you still end up empty because your motives were wrong. Never date and allow anyone to use you in hopes of having love, because all you will really get is sex and a broken heart and sometimes even a pregnancy, you did not plan or expect.

The first prerequisite for qualifying a man in a successful relationship is that he is a God-fearing man. One reason so many marriages are floundering is that the husbands have not prepared themselves spiritually for their task. Now don't be misled by thinking this is something that can be done for an outside show to others. He must truly mean this with his heart, or you and other people will be able to tell. He shouldn't show you attention in public and ignore you in private. A queen is treated the same always!

A virtuous woman knows how to wait for the man God has for her. She accepts nothing less than a real Godly man. In order for this to manifest from the heart of your man, you must respect him and treat him like he's your king. Remember, you reap what you sow, and you should complement each other (1 Thess. 5:11).

Can you stand to be loved?

Growing up, my mom and dad really taught me a lot about self-sufficiency; and after two years into my marriage,

I realized that I needed to share some of my independency-it wasn't easy. You must not allow your-self to become so independent that you can't settle down with a man. Being independent doesn't automatically make you "wife material" some of the most independent ladies make the worst wives. Yes. A real woman can do it by herself....but a real man won't let her! No man wants to fight for the man position in the relationship. To him it's like dating another man trapped in a woman body. Seriously, once you have a man, then it is time to allow him to step up and do his job of properly loving you. Unfortunately, it does not happen like that for many women. Why? They will not step back and allow the man to love them. They try to do everything for themselves — don't get me wrong; I commend and love that you can hold your own. I applaud that you don't make yourself a burden to others and have learned to handle business correctly on your own. The problem is you are making things harder on yourself. You are allowing more stress and mental fatigue to enter your life when it is not always as necessary as you make it seem. Most women have this issue and may not even realize it. It is hindering you in relationships and in even trying to find a relationship. While you must maintain some independence, there must be balance. That man is supposed to be there to lighten the load and help keep you feeling as best as you can. A lot of the men want to help, but your independent woman syndrome causes you to deny his attempts. You not only make it harder for you in the present, but if you have married or end up marrying this guy, you have now set yourself up for more frustration. You are basically programming this man that you can do it on your own. So do not be surprised when he continues to assume "she got this." Most women, if not all women, want a man who can step up, but if every time he tries, you basically tell him to sit down, well guess what he will now automatically do.

Chapter 8

Men want to feel loved as much as women. If he doesn't feel appreciated, valued, respected...he's not going to be happy in the relationship. You have to let a man feel like a man, or you can do some serious damage to him and the relationship. Not to mention, many women who are overly independent also can become very aggressive in how they speak to their man. If you are quick to come at him in a negative way, and are constantly nagging him when he does something you do not like or approve of, then trust there is going to be a problem. Many times a man who is constantly having his manhood crushed by his woman will then look for any opportunity to assert himself and get his manhood back. Unfortunately, men tend to do that at the very wrong time and in not a smart way, which then leads to more issues, but had you not nagged but communicated with him in the first place, well then we could have avoided the whole problem altogether. I am in no way telling you not to be an independent woman. I just want you to learn how to balance being an independent woman, as well as the "Right Woman" for the man you choose to give that honor.

Part 2

BLUEBERRY LETTERS:
REAL TALK ABOUT RELATIONSHIPS...
PRACTICAL, GODLY ADVICE

Chapter 9

Why Do I Always Attract the Wrong Type of Man?

Sometimes rejection ... is for your protection.

Why does it seem like there are only two types of guys I end up with: ones who are too emotional and like me too much or ones who just want sex, not a relationship. It's maddening! I go from one extreme to the other. I always get infatuated with guys who end up playing games with me too. And I get my hopes up and get hurt. I'm so tired of this. Where are the decent guys in this world?

Not all men are sex driven; maybe you're approached that way because that's what your spirit invites. There are plenty of good men in the world, but work on you first by maintaining your standards. Standards keep you from falling into the wrong relationship or situations with the wrong people You don't have to dress sexy to get a man, you don't have to open your legs, you don't have to search; you just need to be a woman of standards. Be the best you that you can be, and you will attract a better quality of man. It's not to say that there won't be the occasional idiot, but when you build your self-worth by being the best person you can be, and then you

Chapter 9

will see more clearly. You may say, "Well, I have been the best me. I always wear heels (except for work) and look decent always." Well, that's great that you look good, but understand that what you look like isn't everything. Are you successful? Are you confident? Are you a good person? More importantly, do you know your own self-worth?

A lot of women get hurt because they don't know the difference between what men like and what men respect. Looks are important, but even more important is how you carry yourself. You are a woman, so obviously you will encounter some idiots, more or less. But the important point is, what can you offer when a genuine man comes? Confidence, good conversation; these are the qualities men generally look for on the first date.

Wrong men will be there. You have to filter those out. And experiences teaches, more or less. Watch out for the red flags.

Your answer may lie in where you go to get these guys, or what you do to get them, or what you do to keep them. When I listen to women who tell me what they want in a guy and what characteristics make a good catch, I just say, "You are headed for trouble." This may sound silly, but talk to your mother, if you can. If not, talk to some older female who is wise. Share your ideas of what you think it takes to get a good man and where you should go to find one.

Yes, the handsome ones get a lot of girls and sex, so they are going to expect that from you. Do not rush yourself into a relationship where you are letting your feelings go too soon. Try to date, and commit to not get serious for six months. That means no sex as well. You will find that a lot of the players will move on quickly if they find that they cannot get sex. That will weed out most of them because you're not willing to settle for just anyone. Hold out a bit until the right one does come along.

You pick; don't let them pick you. Honestly, we all go through times where we think it's never going to get better. When I was younger, my friend once told me I needed to turn off the neon sign on my head that said, "If you are a user or abuser, follow me!" Lol (laugh out loud).

But honestly, follow your heart. It might lead you wrong a time or two, but it's known to have been right a time or two also. Just take a step back, breathe deeply, and really look at your past relationships. Learn from them. Learn to read the signs of the type of guy you don't want to be paired with. That way, instead of being victimized by fate, you can warily determine whether or not a guy is right for you.

Godly men, Mr. Rights, do exist! Quit settling for less than what you're supposed to have. Let him put a ring on it first. Celibacy is not a curse-word. Purity is commendable. God didn't give Adam a girlfriend, and he didn't create Eve to be a side chick, but a wife. When praying for a spouse, here are some biblical qualities that Christians should look for even when they're dating. Remember, the person you date, you could soon someday marry! So, work on your finances together. Get your savings up. Don't go into a marriage struggling, marriages alone aren't easy. Some of the general qualities they should have are as follows:

1. Marry a person of like faith. If a Christian marries a non-Christian, they do not share common values in Christ. God does recognize a marriage to an unbeliever (1 Cor. 7:12–16; 1 Pet. 3:1–2), but such a relationship will present problems that could otherwise be avoided (1 Cor. 7:39; 9:5; 1 Pet. 3:7).

2. Marry someone who wants children (Ps. 127:3, Prov. 31:28; Mal. 2:15; Gen. 9:1; 1 Tim. 2:15). Marriage

is God's way of multiplying the human race, but He wants godly offspring. Before you marry, discuss this subject, and discuss how the children are to be raised. Such things should not be taken for granted, as it will seriously affect the marriage relationship.

3. Marry someone who practice abstinence/a virgin (Song of Sol. 4:12; Gen. 2:23–24). Examine Bible verses that stress virginity, and see the implications. For example, a priest could marry only a virgin (Lev. 21:7–15). Lawful sex pertains to the marriage relationship, and outside of that relationship, it is forbidden — including premarital sex (Song of Sol. 2:7; 8:4). Abstinence before marriage is the wise and godly choice. This does not mean that such sins cannot be forgiven and that marriage is no longer an option.

4. Marry someone who is honest (Prov. 11:1; 13:11). Honesty is a basic measure of character. If a person is not honest, that person cannot be depended upon in any area of life.

5. Marry someone who will be faithful to the relationship (Prov. 2:16–19; 5:3–14; 6:24–33; 7:6–23). Marriage is a covenant relationship (Mal. 2:14–16) and must be respected. Question: can marriage survive infidelity? Yes, but there has to be genuine repentance and forgiveness. There is a difference between having the right to divorce because of infidelity and divorce being required. We should work to keep marriages intact.

6. Marry someone who isn't lazy. This pertains to men and women (Prov. 24:30–34; 31:27; 2 Thess. 3:10). Laziness leads to poverty, dishonesty, and other bad traits.

7. Marry someone who is a good listener. Good communication is a key to a happy marriage. One cannot consider the needs of others unless one is willing to listen (James 1:19). This is how we show that we care. Beware of those who desire only to hear themselves.

8. Marry someone who exhibits love for others (1 Cor.13:4–7).

9. Marry someone whom you love and who loves you (Song of Sol. 8:6–7; Eph. 5:25–29, 33; Titus 2:4).

10. Marry someone who is considerate. The opposite is to be crude and rude (1 Sam. 25:3, 25). This trait comes from an attitude of putting others ahead of self (Phil. 2:3).

11. Do not marry someone who is guilty of physical or mental abuse (Prov. 27:3–4). Ignoring such conduct does not solve the problem. Many wives who are married to abusive husbands become codependent and live in fear and misery.

12. Do not marry someone who has a temper problem (Prov. 19:19; 22:24–25; 27:3). There is no peace for those who associate with such a person.

13. Marry someone who has a sense of humor (Prov. 17:22). Don't take yourself so seriously that you lose your sense of humor. Godly humor is not designed to harm or put down others, but is designed to reduce tension, is appropriate to the occasion, and keeps sadness from becoming overwhelming.

14. Marry someone with whom you share a common background and common interests. The more people have in common, the easier the adjustments will be in marriage.

15. Do not marry someone addicted to drugs or alcohol. Sometimes people get married thinking that love conquers all or that they will rescue or reform their mates. If such people will not change before marriage, what makes you think they will change after marriage?

16. Marry someone who can forgive and accept forgiveness. This is part of what it means to love others.

17. Marry someone who can accept correction or criticism (Prov. 12:1; 13:18). This requires humility and the ability to grow in the grace and knowledge of Christ.

18. Marry a friend (Prov. 17:17; 18:24). Your mate should be someone with whom you can confide and open your heart, one who always has your best interest in mind (Song of Sol. 5:16).

19. Marry someone who is financially responsible. Money issues are a leading reason for divorce.

20. Marry someone who practices good hygiene. Cleanliness is something that we do for others, not just for ourselves. If a person is sloppy in appearance, it will be reflected in other things as well.

21. Marry someone who is optimistic and joyful (Prov. 18:14; Phil. 4:4–7, 11–13).

22. Marry someone who has good self-esteem (Song of Sol. 1:5; 2:1). The Bible teaches that we cannot love others if we do not love ourselves (Matt. 22:39; Eph. 5:28–30).

23. Marry someone who shares the same moral and spiritual values. Someone who defends homosexuality or accepts the doctrines of humanism has no common ground with a Christian (2 Cor. 6:14–19).

24. Marry someone who is a good example to others (1 Tim. 4:8–12). Good character should top any list.

25. Do not marry someone simply for looks (Prov. 11:22; 31:30). To be good looking, a good athlete, a powerful king, or a good lover is no substitute for true love that lasts.

Above all, remember, if you are unhappy with the person you are dating, more than likely you will be unhappy in a serious relationship or marriage with them. You cannot date wrong and marry right.

Chapter 10

"Divorce or Not"
-Married but Depressed

I am a strong woman on the surface, but inside I am in pieces and now struggling with depression. I have been married for five years with no kids (relocated to Georgia and have no family here). I have been with him for a total of seven years, since the age of twenty-two, and I am twenty-nine years old as of July of this year. We had a great sex life before we got married, and he said he wanted more kids (he has kids from a previous marriage.) As soon as we got married, I took off my hair coil, and since then he has refused to sleep with me. I rely on toys and have never cheated on him (but it's been so hard). I work from home; I'm indoors all the time and do not really have friends here. I have come to the conclusion that my hubby does not want kids, because every time I bring up the topic, he gives different excuses (I think he is down-low, really).

I want kids badly, but I'm twenty-nine with no regular income. I just feel this is really the end of my dreams. I am five feet three inches tall, apple figure, depressed.

All my old friends are now married with kids. I am a graduate but never took employment since I had a thriving business, but right now I have no motivation. I just want a family! I've also taken professional courses and hope to get a constant income job soon and move out. But my hubby says I am too old now and no one will want me (he emotionally abuses me, but I am very strong, though I cry behind closed doors).

It's too hard. I am scared that if I leave this marriage, I will not find anyone else; I will be childless and alone. I cannot speak about this to my family because they are far away and would be worried. I just need a strategy to get myself emotionally stable again and then married (to the right person) within a year and have kids.

Well, seems like you knew going in this wasn't a great idea, but you took the chance with him because you loved him. Never leave family behind for a man; family is too significant to me to just up and leave. For those women who are reading this, try to live at least in the same state as your family for the first year, if possible, if you have not known the person for a significant period of time.

I love children very much, and you definitely should plan to have a child someday. But please understand that you're only twenty-nine! There's nothing too hard for God (Gen. 18:14). Sarah was ninety years old when she had a child. My friend just had twins at forty-five years old; they are well and healthy. There is nothing wrong with prolonging when you're just not ready, when you're not ready financially or emotionally.

You want to be the best you before you bring a child into this world. Yes, a child will bring you unconditional love,

Chapter 10

but you must love yourself first. Maybe your desire to have a child is showing way too much, and the fact that you don't have a steady income and that he already has kids could be a deterring factor for him. You can't just want a baby and expect it to happen, if things are not in order. Also, why do you want to have a baby with someone who emotionally abuses you? Why do you want a baby if you are depressed? You need to find out how you can be happy now, before you add another life into the mix.

I don't know, as for you changing careers or whatever you mentioned, you are never too old to start something new. If you do divorce him, make sure to follow through with your plans. I pray for your emotional, physical, financial, spiritual, and mental well-being.

Please stop allowing this person to abuse you. His telling you that you're too old and no one will ever want you are lies! Don't let his negative words destroy you. You're not too old. You're almost in your early thirties, and of course another man will want you. Don't let him feed you garbage.

Verily, verily, I say unto you, you don't need to be a certain size to feel wanted. Both big and skinny women can have men problems. There are men who are attracted to tall, short, big, and small. If you want to lose weight, do it for yourself to be healthier, to feel sexier. Don't worry that all your friends are married with kids; focus on just you. You will have your time one day, too. Don't compare yourself to others; it won't do you any good. Believe that you deserve better, and make that a reality.

I'm not one to condone divorce, but if he is what you describe him as, then yes, do leave the marriage. What good does it do for you to stay in an emotionally abusive marriage?

No good at all. You have already given him seven long years of your life. He's neglecting your needs, he's emotionally closed off, he's belittling, and he won't give you what you desire — a child. Seek professional counsel with him, and both of you need to make the best decision for the relationship before any more damage is done.

Lastly, depression is a serious issue, and it's detrimental to one's psyche and well-being. You know what's causing these negative feelings; therefore, eliminate them from your life. It's never too late to do better for yourself and to start all over. As for your strategy, yes, get a job first so you can save up some money. You will need that whether you stay or leave. Work out and eat well for yourself, and *don't* try to pressure yourself to meet a man by a specific time. Giving yourself a deadline is a really bad idea. You might end up meeting a man who will take advantage of you and leave you even more brokenhearted. Be careful. Yes, children are a blessing, but you have time, so don't rush! Nothing good should be swift and hasty (Phil. 4:6).

Chapter 11

Cougars and Sugar Daddies

For you who are reading this book and asking yourself what a cougar is, let me explain that a cougar/sugar daddy is a man or woman who likes to date younger people, usually twenty years younger or more.

> As a young lady eighteen years old, I have a four-year-old child. The older man (sugar daddy) and I just started talking, and surprisingly, we have a lot in common. But this age thing is really bothering me. I don't look my age, so people don't question us. We don't talk about our age gap, but I think about it all the time. I feel like, why bother getting serious if it's never going to work out? My friends say just get the money and see where the relationship takes me.
>
> There were several issues, like his drinking all the time, he has a 10 year old child and his not being emotionally supportive was a big one that started the rest of it off. There were many other times when he thought I was wrong about something. Many times I would get a speech about him having more years on earth than me, etc. Also, his phrasing for many

things wasn't great. There were times when he also frightened me because of what he wanted at that time (he's in a different stage of life), and I wasn't there yet. I would hear stories of him and his friends going here or there and doing different things. He had completed things I hadn't even begun to do yet. He had been there, done that, got tired of it, and didn't want it anymore. Should I be serious about this type of relationship?

Of course not! No respecting man would want a woman that young. You're still a teenager. Love to you is an emotion, a good woman and man to you is just an idea. You don't know as much as you think you know. He's down with it because he's just happy to have fun with a naive young girl. He has a child; it says a lot about him that he's not with his baby's mother (not to pass judgment on him, but you have to pay attention to little details). Take it easy messing with older men. You'll find yourself in predicaments you wish you weren't in.

Forget this "you only live once" stuff. Yeah, it's true that you only live once, but the relationship that God wants you to have, although it might require you to surrender some things, will never require you to surrender who you are, your dreams, your dignity, or your self-respect. Find someone your age, or just chill and find another hobby.

You think that you have a lot in common, but keep talking to him and you'll realize that you have a lot less in common than you think. Just take things slow— real slow. I wouldn't automatically dismiss him because of his age, but be prayerful and pay attention to some red flags. Just remember, you are only eighteen. So don't make the mistake of getting tied down, and definitely don't get pregnant. The more you keep making the same mistakes, the more they'll cost you.

Chapter 12

Abortion

I am five weeks pregnant. The condom split, and I took the morning-after pill seven hours later when I woke up; but that obviously didn't work. The father is my boyfriend, who is very anti-abortion. When I was freaking out the day after, he said in an event where I accidentally fell pregnant, we could get married before the baby arrived (for family), and he would support me and be with me every step of the way. He has a strong sense of responsibility and a can-do attitude, so he genuinely believed we would have to just accept it and work our hardest. He has always said, "I will never let my girlfriend abort my child."

I am in no way emotionally, financially, or mentally ready for a baby. I am working till I go back to the university next year, and he has started a graduate job. I come from a very troubled home, and I want to be able to have children when I can fully love and cherish them. Right now I can't, and I can't bring a human being to earth knowing that I'm not ready. I really don't want to tell my boyfriend, as this will tear us apart. He will never let me have an abortion, so I think it's best I just don't tell anyone and do it secretly. Help!

First, I must say you must ensure there's a long-term commitment (I recommend marriage) before you commit to intimacy with someone. However, frankly, lots of women say they aren't ready for children and parenthood. Babies happen. I was married when my first came — not necessarily by accident, because I know there is always a potential for pregnancy during intimacy. Sure, my circumstances are different from yours, but the point I'm making is that life happens, and expect the unexpected. You have a relationship (I hope) built on trust with your boyfriend. Can you honestly hold such news from him? You both created a life, and he does have a right to know. No relationship lasts with such secrets because eventually the truth always comes out — always.

You also have the option to have the child and give it up for adoption. Please consider this carefully as well. If you truly don't want this child, and you want to respect your boyfriend's feelings, then adoption really is the best option. Lastly, you are stronger than you think. Don't sell yourself short. Sure, having a child is a huge responsibility, but it's not the end of the world. Children bring immense joy into one's life. Please consider talking to people who really know you and your situation, and make a decision then after you have received much counsel (Prv 15:22).

Chapter 13

Overcoming Molestation

I was molested by a family member, abused and raped by my father. Now I feel the need to punish men for the pain of my rape and past sexual abuse. Lately, out of bitterness, resentment, and an inability to forgive, I have become sexually promiscuous and even lesbian in an effort to fulfill my mind-set of "there are no good men" and "men do it, so why can't women?" My pain is associated with men; because of my bitterness, I hate and am distrustful of all men. I have been with over thirty men and three women, and half of those were within a one- year span of deep resentment and anger. How do I move on?

As one can imagine, sexual abuse and rape are very painful and can cause various other issues. Please don't live your life scarred or playing the victim. Each time you think about, talk about, or remember the pain of your past, you put that energy squarely in the middle of your life right now. What is most important is that you forgive the other person and make the necessary corrections about yourself through prayer; God is the comfort you see, the guidance that you need, the healing you have prayed for. This fulfillment cannot come from a man-you will make many bad decisions out of loneliness or hurt because you are looking for love in the wrong places. God has healing waiting for you once you admit you need Him and have the courage to seek help. The beginning of your healing, as difficult as it might seem, is forgiveness. Matthew 6:14–15, in the Amplified Bible says, "For if you forgive people their trespasses [their reckless and willful sins, leaving them, letting them go and giving up resentment], your heavenly Father will also forgive you. But if you do not forgive others their trespasses [their reckless and willful sins, leaving them, letting them go and giving up resentment], neither will your Father forgive you your trespasses."

There is a process involved when healing from trauma. It is important to understand that it is not the same for everyone. We all heal at our own rate, and we cannot judge others or ourselves in that process. Be patient. There is not a point when we should say, "Just get over it." There is, in fact, no real getting over it, but there is a point when it no longer has the same power over us (Rom. 8:37). You have to trust in God. God will deal with whoever truly hurt you, if you put it in His hands through forgiveness (or if you hurt them).

Forgiving is a seed of obedience to His Word. When you forgive, you allow God to heal your heart. You live a healthier life free of the poison of unforgiveness. The stress of walking in unforgiveness hinders your faith and blocks your blessings. How can you ask God to forgive you, yet you can't forgive and sow mercy unto another? Unforgiveness nested in your heart will slowly destroy your life. The seed of unforgiveness roots itself in other areas of your life and causes deeper issues. Naturally, when something happens to you that hurt, it's just as fresh in your mind as if it had just happened.

Chapter 13

No matter the degree or level of pain, you have to let go, forgive yourself, and forgive the person. Continuing to live in this poison of unforgiveness torments your life. Matthew 18:23–25 teaches that when you don't forgive people, you get turned over to the torturer, meaning that you have thoughts of hate or feelings of bitterness swimming in your mind. When you walk in forgiveness, you help yourself. I know for many of you the thought of forgiving someone who has molested you is hard. You are thinking, "Hey, I got all the pain, and he/she has moved on!" In your mind, you feel you are in a cage, while the abuser has total freedom. You also help the other person when you forgive because you are releasing that person to God. You have to get out of the way so God can do His work (Luke 17:2).

The Bible says the truth will set you free. God will make sure to get the appropriate truths revealed to you so you can fully understand some of the dysfunctional behavior that was occurring in your family and help separate truth from error so you do not fall victim to the same type of distorted and warped thinking in your adult life. When God wants us to learn how to fully let the past go, I believe He targets more of the bad things in our past, especially the things that will really play with our minds and emotions where our hearts can start to harden and our thinking become distorted, warped, and unhealthy.

We also have many good things from our past. We all have a certain amount of treasured memories that we will never forget. God wants us to keep all of these good memories fully intact (Phil 4:8). There is no harm in going back down memory lane from time to time with many of the good things that occurred in your past. The road to healing is difficult. It is filled with dips, mountains, and twists, but the good news is, whether you believe it in the beginning or along the way, there really is good that will come out of this (Rom. 8:28). There will come a day when suddenly you know you were not to blame, and you are safe, powerful, and the most courageous overcomer!

Chapter 14

I Want My Man to Be Happy

So, my husband is feeling pretty down because of some work-related incidents. Do you have any suggestions of things I could do for him that could cheer him up, make him feel better? He's an awesome man, and I'd like to spoil him a bit, make him feel appreciated, show him he's still number one in my book no matter what. I hesitate to buy him anything because I'm scared that spending money on him could have an opposite effect, maybe make him feel even worse. I'd appreciate some help as to what you'd want your woman to do in this situation.

The best thing you can do is to appeal to the things about him you know he likes. Women love when they receive gifts or attention that caters specifically to them as individuals (for example, a favorite meal, an item they mentioned offhandedly that they wanted during idle conversation, a favorite beauty or spa-treatment product, going to a favorite night spot, a date night, encouragement to catch up with some of their friends they haven't been able to catch up with for a while, or simply just time set aside to relax and be waited on while catching up with some of their favorite TV shows). It works both ways.

Support his goals. A man needs to know you believe in him. Find ways to move him towards his goals. Consider sacrificing a date night to work with him on tasks that will help him accomplish his goals. Consider saving money to purchase tools or resources that will be helpful for him. I can't tell you what it may be for your man, but part of what makes you a good woman is when you understand your man. Show him appreciation by giving him something that you know he wants, and you will know what is better than anyone else. Even small things, like random kisses and hugs, tell him you care or love him. I don't know your husband, but try to avoid over-the-top elaborate gestures when a guy is feeling down. It's the small and often unsaid things that count the most. Sometimes we just want to rant and want a sounding board. In those times, we won't be looking to you for an answer, but we just need to talk to someone about the situation.

My Man Doesn't Seem Interested

My boyfriend has not given me much attention lately; it has been this way for about two weeks. It seems like he doesn't care if we talk. In the past, he would get mad when I fell asleep on him and left him up alone. We have been together for ten months, and I try to talk to him, but his responses lately have been short and impersonal. He doesn't even call me "baby" anymore or greet me with a kiss like he always did in the past.

I hate to say it, but it sounds like he's lost interest or he's not feeling good about the relationship. It could be temporary or permanent, but I wouldn't be the one to stay around if I were being mistreated. Try to see if you can have

Chapter 14

a conversation with him first before jumping to conclusions. If he hasn't given you any reason to think otherwise, give him the benefit of the doubt. If his answers don't suffice, it may be time to move on. Don't try to analyze the answers he gives or try to make excuses if what he says isn't what you deserve. Count your blessings and bid him adieu. On the flip side, he is human, and sometimes we just need time to collect our thoughts. So just hear him out and go from there.

Chapter 15

One-Sided Attractions

A middle-aged woman had a crush on a handsome young Christian man, caught feelings, and began obsessing over him over and over again, creating an illusion of a fairy-tale love in her head. Her question is, "How do I let go of a guy who doesn't reciprocate my feelings? How do I let go of a guy that I didn't actually have a relationship with?" In essence, how does she let go of a one-sided attraction that in her mind has created a relationship out of her feelings?

For a start, you can't break up when there is nothing to break up from. The only person you have to break up with is you and your rather overactive imagination and feelings. The issue here isn't really about him, as he's not really part of the equation when you've created an illusion rather than keeping your feet in the real world. The issue is about you and the fact that you don't want to let go of your feelings, your obsession, your drama and loneliness. There are four key reasons why these situations come about:

Chapter 15

1. You are a queen of projection.

You choose men who cater to your own negative self-fulfilling prophecy and are likely to leave you "crushing" on them. Then you project the feelings that you think you have on them and assume that because you think you feel a certain way about them, they should feel that way about you too. You want them to notice you, to see you in the way that you see them, and you conduct the great majority of this stuff in your head without communicating it to them and then wonder why they haven't reciprocated your feelings.

2. You think that your feelings are big enough for the two of you.

You lose all sense of proportion and become so consumed with how you feel that you want him to be swept up in all the love you have to give. You think that one day he'll catch up to how you feel and return it. Trust me, men don't do this.

You don't actually want to be in a relationship. You're living in a dream world and afraid of being rejected in the real world. In choosing men who are aloof and unlikely to be interested in you, you get to avoid having to be hurt in a way that you're trying to avoid. Instead, you build sand castles in the sky in your head and then feel rejected by your own daydreams. The reality is that you need some sort of inspiration for these illusions, and he is not a part of your life. You're very emotionally unavailable.

3. You don't want to let go.

As many of us have discovered, even if it's the most toxic thing to continue feeling as we do or being involved with someone, we continue, not only because it's a bit like "I've started, so I'll finish," but also because even when there is nothing or it's not really worth your time, we don't want to let go. You don't want to get real with yourself in case you find that you have something difficult or painful to look at. You don't want to admit that you can often be the creator of your own pain; and you certainly don't want to admit that you're letting go of something that didn't exist, and even if it did exist, it was for the most part in your head.

Remember, it's difficult to make someone accountable for something that is a grand illusion in your head, when you could have been making them accountable for real behavior. Likewise, you can't wonder why someone is not feeling what you want them to feel when they're not part of the relationship in your head. These men end up acting as inspiration for your latest round of feelings. It's like they put in some input at the beginning, and then you just took it from there, refusing to acknowledge whether they are even there or not, whether they are behaving in line with what's in your head, and if not, why not?

Quite frankly, any misery you are feeling is for the most part your own creation, because you are not interested in keeping your feet in reality, and have been too busy wallowing in your own world. In doing this, you're not seeing signs that you need to get real, and you're not hearing signs that you need to get real. In fact, the man may have no clue that you are even interested in him, or if he does, he may have told you that he's not interested and you switched to unreciprocated-feelings mode and hovered there, expecting him to see you in the way that you want to be seen and magically catch up with your feelings. It doesn't matter what he feels; you're interested only in the fact that you feel what you feel, and you want him to feel that too.

Chapter 15

The thing is, from the moment you recognize that (1) you are not having your feelings reciprocated or that (2) you're not in a relationship with this man, major warning signals should be going through your brain that there is something seriously wrong if you are still trying to get him to reciprocate and obsessing about him over an extended period of time. It's one thing to have a crush, and it's another thing to allow your-self to participate in a self-destructive pursuit of pain and then blame it on someone else. If you have made the choice to continue loving and chasing him, with much of it taking place in your head as you wait for crumbs or nothing at all, you're on a serious avoidance mission. It's like you want to hide away on these self-created feelings of rejection rather than get out there in the real world and risk yourself in a real relationship.

While I recognize that in some instances you can be misled by a guy to believe that he feels more than he does, I tend to find that women who are in this situation are invariably in it because they decided that they were crazy about someone and don't want to let that and the fantasy go. You've decided that you want him, love him, and regardless you'll find a way to show him that he should notice and love you too. You're going to ride this imaginary horse of love till it collapses. You're back at the juncture again where you think that deciding that you love or feel something about someone creates an automatic IOU. You're also back at that juncture where you love without any foundation for loving and then refuse to opt out because you don't want to let go of the fantasy or the illusion and get real and deal with your problems.

Trust me, if you're doing this, you have some big issues to deal with because you're engaging in incredibly self-destructive behavior and repeatedly creating a rejection situation for yourself and then wondering why you're in pain. It's because you did it — not him! In all honesty, the only way these situations end is when *you* end it. You don't need to say anything because, to be honest, I think some of these men would be a touch confused if you told them that something was over that they didn't think had started.

Stop calling, stop chasing, stop texting, stop seeing a bread loaf when there is barely a crumb. Stop waiting, stop hoping, stop projecting, and stop the madness. Stop creating drama and then wondering why you are miserable. It's all one-sided; you are the master orchestrator of your own soap opera. Commit yourself to the Lord (Ps. 22:8).

Take things at face value so that when he doesn't call, it's because he doesn't want to speak with you, not because he's waiting for you to make a move. When you don't hear from him for months, it's not because you did something wrong that you need to figure out; it's because you are not in a relationship, and while you are daydreaming your life away, he is out there living his. Yes, that's right, living — and if you spend your energy wanting men who don't want you and then obsessing about why they don't want you, your life will be at one mega standstill.

If you point-blank cannot accept that (1) it's for the most part in your head, (2) if he doesn't want you, then it's time to start learning to stop wanting him, and (3) you're creating your own drama and pain, then you must at least accept that you are 100 percent responsible for where you are now and don't get to let yourself off the hook and blame him. Then go and talk to someone because spending your life and brain time escaping from the real world while hurting yourself and not wanting that to change says that it's time you spoke to someone and got to the heart of your issues.

Chapter 15

But if you are at that point where you want to and can do something about this, don't try to make things any more complicated than they are, because when you let go of something that doesn't and didn't exist, you have that power and are in the driver's seat of what happens to you. Don't make out like he has to do something to end this; you have to do something and cold turkey it out so that you can gain some real perspective and get to the heart of why you are engaging in this self-destructive behavior, so that you don't go back.

Chapter 16

My Baby's Daddy is Crazy

I came home from a weekend out of town to find my apartment completely empty. My clothes, makeup, food, cleaning supplies, shoes, birth certificate, bank statements, textbooks, and tampons were all gone. All that was left was my furniture. Someone climbed up my fire escape, broke my window, and stole my spare key. I know it was my ex(my baby's daddy), whom I broke up with over six months ago. Anything with his name or picture on it he took. Also, on the way out of town, I saw him. He asked me where I was going and I lied, but he knew I was going far because I was at the airport. I called the police, but there were no fingerprints and no witnesses.

I don't have enough money right now to replace even a quarter of what was stolen. I don't have any family in the area. I feel so bad. I was trying to better my life by letting him go and finishing school and finding a new job, but then this happened. My landlord refuses to change the locks, so I have to do that myself. Most of the stuff he took was replaceable, but I still feel so violated.

Chapter 16

First of all, don't feel or act like you have to seek revenge. The Bible teaches us God will bring us our justice. He knows what was done to you and what you have done to others. "God will repay the exact compensation owed to us. He will settle and solve the offenses of his people." (Heb. 10:30). So don't go handling this on your own. There's no need to fight or have anyone fight him for you — that's horrible advice. That's how things escalate. Let the law enforcement handle this situation.

Be persistent and keep calling them until they give in. Tell them that you're missing class because you need your textbooks; be consistent with it until they send an officer over to his place to talk to him. File a police report. Stay with a friend for now (since you mentioned not having family). Don't stay alone in your place because who knows what is his agenda? If he can do this to an ex, he cannot be trusted. He may return, and that's unsafe.

Chapter 17

I'm Feeling Low-Self-Esteem

I was once in a verbally abusive relationship, until I met my current boyfriend. Lately my boyfriend has made me feel like I'm replaceable. I'm quite positive the longer I feel this way, the sooner it will ruin our relationship. It's my fault for asking questions I know I can't handle the answer to, such as "What do I lack?" He tells me I'm not adventurous and cease to have fun when something seems even slightly dangerous, which maybe is not fair to him because he really likes doing outgoing things.

Then I made things worse by saying, "So it's possible for you to find a woman who offers you the things that I lack?" He stated, "Yes, but I want you. So you don't have to worry about that." This answer didn't make me feel any better, and weeks later I'm feeling low self-esteem. It's made me become the annoying, suspicious girlfriend, which I hate. I don't like checking his phone or Facebook (he's aware of me doing these things). I'm sure this does not help but only makes matters worse; no one wants to be with someone who invades their privacy, I'm certain.

Chapter 17

I'm not excited about him starting summer classes this semester. I keep thinking he's going to meet some adventurous broad who fears nothing and have the greatest time with her. Please advise.

Well, if he hasn't given you any reason to suspect he's cheating and if he truly treats you well, then try not to jeopardize a good thing. You also do not want to appear to lack confidence or insecure. Don't think negatively about yourself; call yourself what you truly are. You are a child of God (Prov. 3:15, more precious than rubies), and He loves you. All godly men want to be with someone who feels good about herself and feels irreplaceable and worth being loved. Then try to bend a little and participate in things he enjoys, no matter how boring. He's with you for a reason: he enjoys your company. You'll be fine.

I also think that you need to compromise a little. Start gradually doing little things that he is interested in, and then participate more as time goes on. At least show him that he is important enough for you to make an attempt, instead of just shooting it down as soon as he mentions it. I don't know you, but it sounds like you may have some self-esteem issues, which is why you asked those questions in the first place. If that's the case, then counseling would not hurt, because your self-esteem issues may have come from your verbally abusive relationship. Some people say when you go looking for trouble, you'll find it, so be careful with that because you open the door to so many other problems. How would you feel if he was going through your things? You are giving the green light and setting a precedent by going through his.

Please don't dwell just on the negative, but glow in your positives and think about what you can do to overcome or change some of the negatives, as long as it's within reason.

I also don't think you should change yourself for anyone, but compromising to enhance or better a relationship, yes. For example, you might not be a person who likes action-packed movies and he does, while you like chick flicks and of course he probably doesn't. But sometimes it's okay to watch that action-packed, has-no-meaning movie with him, and he in return will watch a sappy chick flick with you every now and then.

I don't think that's changing who you are; that's working together to make the relationship successful. Sometimes we do things we don't necessarily like for someone that we love when we know they would do it for us. God led him to you, right? He's with you right? So like I said, focus on your positives. *Negative* may not even be the best word. Let's say-use your areas of improvement, as just that. I'm sure he has some areas to work on; we all do.

Anybody can be replaceable at any given time. No one is above that, but I don't think that's your issue. These are simple fixes. Never let something that's good to and for you get away over something that could be worked on and improved with time.

And I'm even going to say these aren't serious deal breakers, because if so, he would be gone by now. I personally don't think he is asking too much, just pick and choose your battles; this one seems like an easy win for you! Also, if a man wants to cheat on you, he will, regardless of what you are doing. You can be adventurous, an iron chef in the kitchen, and everything else, and a man will still cheat on you if that's what he wants to do.

That's why it's important to allow God to choose your relationships. What I mean by that is when God sends you

Chapter 17

something or someone, it adds to you, supplements you, promotes positive results, and does not deduct or subtract or bring consistent negativity (Prov. 10:22). Don't consume yourself with things you don't have any control over. Nobody wants to be cheated on, but unfortunately, we can't control other people.

Chapter 18

I Have Trust Issues

I'm twenty-five years old but afraid to truly commit to guys because of trust issues in the past. When I say truly commit, I mean, put my all into it (that's hard because of the drama I had with my ex-boyfriend). I literally attract only losers; well, the guys I did like were losers. It seems like they just wanted to jump into intercourse too quickly. Some had girlfriends that I didn't know about, or they were just liars. I cannot lower my standards to accept that type of behavior in a relationship, not that I regret it, but I always end up alone. I'm starting to wonder if it is true that your attraction is a reflection of who you are, because if so, I need to make some changes to myself.

I really hate it when my friends tell me I need to start giving people chances over and over again, but that's just not me. And they also say being single is not cute anymore for my age, but I'm starting to think that maybe I'm not a relationship-type person, or maybe I'm too young to look this deeply into relationships. I can honestly say I do enjoy being in a relationship, but

Chapter 18

I refuse to be mistreated, and I'm always suspicious of every man I meet. Please advise.

What you are feeling is natural. You're only twenty-five, and you still have plenty of time for a relationship. Most of the men you've dated, if they're the same age as you, aren't fully mature yet. They may try their best, but eventually they stumble along the way. What you're going through right now will benefit the man who is lucky enough to win your heart and hopefully make you his wife someday, and what he is going through or has been through will benefit you. You have to go through some heartbreak and make some mistakes in your early relationships before you finally get it right; just focus on yourself and continue to live your life.

Those friends who are in relationships — how are those relationships? Are they healthy? Any woman can have a man if she really wants one, but not every woman needs to have a man every moment of her life. Some women and men suffer from the "can't be by myself" syndrome and end up taking whatever they can get to have someone on their side. Too many people settle for unhealthy relationships. Everybody's plan is different. Just because your friends *think* they've found their soul mates doesn't mean you have to.

I've never heard anyone say that being single at twenty-five is not cute. That is crazy and shows where their priorities are. Also, I will say that you seem sad to me. That is the feeling that you may give off to people, and no one (man or woman) wants a person who appears insecure, sad, desperate, etc., not that I'm calling you desperate. Everyone has insecurities; you just have to be careful how you handle those insecurities, and are you doing something to help you overcome them? When they say you attract what you give off, well, if guys sense an insecure, scared woman, they will come at you and try to take advantage of that or not take you seriously.

I applaud you for not giving in to any man. I think once you start to turn your thought process around, become more positive, look at being single differently, then your light will shine bright and will attract the right type of man. I know that you are a praying woman. So pray for peace of mind and guidance. Do you volunteer, or are you involved in other activities where you can give back? That may help boost you in knowing that you are helping others. Your feelings are normal, and many people go through the same stuff. So don't feel like you are the only one. Sometimes when you forget it and stop thinking about it is when it happens.

Furthermore, if God blesses you with your soul mate, He wants to make sure you are ready to receive him. The person you're meant to be with will never have to be chased, begged, or given an ultimatum. If you have to jump through endless hoops to be with someone, it's probably not the relationship God intended for you. Happiness isn't found by chasing relationships, paychecks or people, but by *chasing God* (Matt. 6:33). Keep your faith, and God will add to you the man who deserves your heart.

Chapter 19

I Feel Like Giving Up on My Marriage

For the last year or so, I've been feeling overwhelmed. I'm a mother of two; my husband is going to make me go crazy. He is always bad-mouthing me to anyone who will listen, I feel judged by everyone, and my feelings are always dismissed. The excuse is he had no mother, or what he did was in the past. He talks to women inappropriately behind my back. He calls my family members and his, which I don't get along with. I'm always honest and open with him, and he turns around and hides many secrets that keep popping up. When they negatively affect our family, he shrugs it off and never tries to understand my perspective.

I'm really stressed and overwhelmed. Even when I try to talk to my mom, she doesn't want to get involved. I'm drowning in this marriage. My husband's compliments for me are, sarcastically-"My wife is a nuisance." He displayed this same type of behavior before, when we had our first child, and he left me. It seems as if he's repeating himself again.

I don't know what to do. I can't stay with him, out of respect for myself, because I feel betrayed. I want to leave with my kids, but I have no family support, and I just gave birth less than two months ago. I feel like he's getting worse because everyone keeps saying, "Where can she go?" I don't know what I can do, but I need some new living arrangements. Please help.

First of all, don't stop praying (1 Thess. 5:17)! I know you are in a very difficult situation, but I don't believe leaving is your best option. Even if your husband seems to be a complete jerk, I strongly suggest you seek some marital counseling first. You can repair or restore your relationship if both of you do the hard work it takes to get your marriage back on track. I've been there, done that, and counseling saved my marriage. You can either get it through your health insurance or possibly a local church that you are a member of. The "Focus on the Family" website also has a list of counselors in your area that you can contact. Explain to your husband that you and he both need to do this if you want a loving, trusting relationship again.

All things are possible through Christ. Even though I never advise people to stay in a relationship just because they have kids together, it isn't fair either to just take the kids and leave. When kids are involved, this is a difficult situation. If you decide to leave, you still need to figure out a way for him to be able to see his kids. Kids depend on both parents for different reasons. If children are used to living with both parents and then are taken away from one (versus being abandoned), it affects them a lot. Kids do not like to be in the position to choose. They know when Mom and Dad are going through things, and the kids should not have to suffer because of Mom and Dad's disagreements, especially if the father is very present and active in their lives.

Chapter 19

If you take the kids and leave, you will have to feel the guilt when your children keep asking for their dad and to talk to their daddy. I'm not saying the kids shouldn't go with you, but that you need to first have a plan in place that works so they won't be kept from their father during this time either — whether it is a family member who will allow you to drop the kids off so he can pick them up and you not cross paths with him, or a lawyer to set up a custody schedule. It is just important for you to plan your move, not just up and leave, because that could lead to more and more chaos. Again, do not make hasty decisions.

First, you should seek legal advice and ask what your options are. Second, you need a plan. That way it won't get too out of hand and messy. And after that, if you really *must* leave, think one step further. List all the stuff you are going to need in order to survive and provide a good living for your kids:

1. Income

2. Place to stay

3. Support from your family

4. Who will look after the kids when you go back to work?

5. Safety for you and your kids

6. Draw up a contract about coparenting with your hubby while you are thinking about divorce. Get him to sign it.

7. Filing for child support and spousal support

8. Filing for divorce

9. If you have any text messages, e-mails, or Facebook messages where he was talking bad about you, or messages he sent to you where he was threatening or swearing at you, gather them together and keep them safe because you will need them during your divorce in court.

10. Whatever you do now, *pray* and cover yourself.

11. Kids need to see their dad. Have a coparenting or parallel parenting plan as soon as possible. I suggest you keep both kids with you. Do not separate your children. If he's bad-mouthing you, chances of him brainwashing the children are very high.

12. As a mother, protect your kids, but never bad-mouth their father, and never take out your frustration on them. Kids are innocent, and they don't deserve to go through such an emotionally wrecking thing like divorce or separation. Remember 1 Thessalonians 5:17 and don't stop praying!

Chapter 20

I'm a Victim of Domestic Violence

My husband and I have been together for seven years, and I keep telling myself every fight is the last one. I know I'm not always innocent in the arguing, but he just takes it to a horrible place. He purposely provokes me, and then as I become angry and the argument escalates, he threatens me, pushes me, calls me names, makes fun of me, and sometimes hits me. I keep saying that one day I'll know when I've had enough, and I'll leave him. But when will that day come? He calls me every nasty name in the book you can think of, and it's so hurtful every time. I'm on this constant roller coaster with him. I'm not sure why I stay in it. It hurts because I often wonder how somebody who supposedly cares about me can treat me so horribly. Then, in every fight, he makes everything seem like it's my fault. He will admit he has problems, and he knows he's messed up, but then he'll go and start an argument again! I'm exhausted and wondering when enough is enough.

The longer the abuse continues, the worse it will get. To hit *anyone* is against the law. No matter what he tells you, the way he is treating you is not only wrong, but it is also against the law. If you can do so safely, start reading about those who have fled abuse. At the very least, tell yourself that you do have options, and start believing in *you* and yourself.

Do not allow him to pull you into arguments. Men like him thrive on seeing you angry and hurting. What they cannot stand to see is strength. Do not hit back, but send a message and leave, if only for a few days, to breathe and start making an escape plan. It takes time, but your life can start over. I left an abusive girlfriend years ago by visiting a friend for the weekend, and I never went back. You can find strength when you are away from the constant verbal abuse. Start thinking of yourself and what you want to do with *your* life. Life is too short to live in abuse. These kinds of people rarely change. There is no reason for them to change because they know that being angry and abusive helps them get their own way. Don't be afraid. You can be strong and escape.

This is a cycle that you want to break before it starts. After abuse, comes a honeymoon phase. In the honeymoon phase of the cycle, the abuser may promise to stop the abuse or to get professional help. He may ask for forgiveness or apologize profusely. He may also try to win you back with presents, favors, or charming behavior in an attempt to maintain his control over you. Then, comes a building up of tensions and then another abusive incident. The cycle repeats itself over and over, and its severity may increase each time.

Unfortunately, the honeymoon phase usually doesn't last. Without intervention and help by a domestic-violence specialist, the abuse doesn't usually stop. Things may deteriorate to the point that you are walking on eggshells as you see the abuser's attitude and behavior worsen again. Eventually abuse erupts in a violent incident, and the cycle repeats.

Chapter 20

In 1 Samuel 24 and 26, David wisely did not just blindly trust Saul's promises, confessions, and apologies. He cautiously kept a safe distance from Saul, waiting to see fruits of repentance (Matt. 7:15–16). He quickly found that Saul was merely going through the honeymoon phase of the cycle of violence. You should not feel obligated to immediately trust the abuser, until he has proven his sincerity. In Matthew 10:16, Jesus tells us we are like sheep among wolves and must be as wise as serpents.

Psychologists have developed a scale called the *continuum of violence* to show how abuse grows over time. This scale lists abusive actions, starting with the less severe and progressing to extreme abuse and death. The escalation of abuse might be so gradual that it is difficult for the victim to see what is happening until the abuse has become quite severe. Or she may learn to cope and accept it, becoming numb to the signs of danger. Without intervention and specialized help, abuse will rarely cease on its own. Often it worsens over time, becoming more severe and more frequent. Many abusers find that wanting or promising to stop is not enough. With specialized domestic-violence programs, hard work, commitment, and accountability, some abusers can change their behavior.

It is important to understand that the behavior listed on the continuum-of-violence scale is called sin in the Bible. It is no wonder that abuse tends to escalate, since sin is a slippery slope that leads to destruction. Praise God that we have a Savior who can change hearts and renew the minds of those who will humble themselves before Him, sincerely repent, and turn from their evil ways.

The continuum of abuse illustrates how physical, psychological, sexual, and social abuse can progress in harm and danger.

Physical abuse (in order of increasing danger): holding down; blocking; pinning; pushing or shoving; shaking or jerking; slapping and bruising; throwing objects; punching; kicking; black eyes, cuts, and chipped teeth; burning with hot drinks, cigarettes, etc.; causing serious falls; choking; severe beatings; broken bones; hitting with objects; back injuries; paralysis; internal injuries; use of weapons; death.

Psychological abuse (in order of increasing severity and danger): "jokes" or put-downs that demean the victim; acting like the victim's feelings, needs, and ideas don't matter; enforcing rigid roles and rules for women; controlling through jealousy; isolating the victim; insults and name-calling; yelling and raging; humiliation; throwing food; fist through wall; threats and intimidation; destruction of her property; hurting or killing pets; displaying guns or sleeping with guns; depriving the victim of sleep; threatening suicide or trying to get the victim to commit suicide; threatening to kill her or the children; death.

Sexual abuse (in order of increasing severity and danger): anger at women, sexual jokes and put-downs, embarrassing comments, treating the woman like a sexual object, sex expected as a duty, withholding sex to punish, touching victim in ways that feel uncomfortable, promiscuity and sexual affairs, sex after or together with violence or abuse, forcing the victim by violence or threats to perform sexual acts the victim doesn't want to do, marital rape, incest with children, sadism, death of victim.

You asked, "Which fight is the last one?" You must decide in your situation that the last one will *not* be when he kills you. Please don't let that be your last fight! Be stronger than most, and get out before you lose the ability to make a decision on how to get out and stay out.

Chapter 21

It's Time for an Upgrade

We have been friends for ten years. We have messed around from time to time but have never been in a relationship. He is really good to me; whenever I need him, he is right there. He will do anything for me without my asking. I'm thirty-five years old, and I have never, ever in my life had a man do for me with no questions, not wanting anything in return. I feel like he loves me, of course, but every time I try to talk about taking the relationship to the next level, it's like he doesn't take me seriously, and I can't seem to finish the conversation with him, out of fear, I guess. Yesterday I asked him if he was ready to commit, and he said, "I thought I was already committed."

I said, "No, for real, to become my real boo." Then he started joking about how we both have too much bad luck and how we were going to be two bad-luck folks together, so I dropped the conversation, and we went on to talk about other things.

I just don't know if he wants me like that. So I have begun to say things like, "I know you love me," or

"You do love me," when he's does something nice for me. Then he just laughs, but I don't know what to do. I want him. Should I just come out and ask him? Should I have another talk and be more forward with him about how I feel?

Yes, you should talk with him again and be very candid about your feelings. If you think he is taking you as a joke, and you've been forming a pattern of joking about it by not making it known how serious you truly are, the first step is to make sure that he knows you're serious.

The next thing to do is to encourage open and honest feedback on his perspective. The reason you need to encourage this is because you want the truth. If he does care about you, he may try to tell you what you want to hear or avoid telling you what he thinks you don't want to hear in an effort to spare your feelings.

You do have to consider the real possibility that because you two have such a good relationship as it is, he may not be interested in trying to fix something that in his eyes is not broken. He very well may have strong feelings for you but be unwilling to take the risk of losing everything that you have or jeopardizing the future you two would have had if things don't work out when you switch to a serious, committed romance.

Either way, since you guys are really tight, all you have to do is talk it out. Respect the honesty, regardless of whether he wants the same thing you want or not; otherwise, you could end up causing unnecessary drama.

Chapter 22

He and I — and the Baby

I've been dating my boyfriend for a couple of years, and I found out that someone is pregnant by him. He claims he slept with her just once. I'm so confused because I'm so in love with him. I need your advice, please. Should I leave him or continue with the relationship?

It's so easy to say that you should leave, but your reaction is different when you are actually in that situation. With that said, I have to say that it's really in your best interest to just leave. First off, you are not married. Under no other circumstance should a woman even consider staying with a man who fathered a child with someone else, unless he is her husband. The key word here is *consider*, and if you are absolutely adamant about staying, you need to leave him at least for a while and pray about the issue. Just staying with a man like that ultimately shows that you are a doormat and that he can do whatever and you won't leave, not even for a second. Please leave. Show him that you are worth more than what he is offering, which is nothing but possible STDs since he is having sex with other women.

In this time, you will find so much out about yourself that you may not even need him or want to be with him. It also allows you to see that maybe there is someone out there who is better for you. If you decide to stay, consider that this can ruin your self-esteem. You will constantly have to think about it. His new child will interrupt the life that you have created as a couple. You will have "baby mama drama." It's just not worth it for someone that you've been with for only a little more than a year and the girl is almost due. He has hidden this from you for quite some time and is just now deciding to be honest.

Another reason to consider is that he cheated and endangered your life by not using protection, impregnated someone else, and then looked you in your face while keeping this secret for months. He seems not to value your relationship, so why should you? You need to be with someone who loves you enough to not betray your trust and endanger your life.

Chapter 23

Relationship Tips

Relationship Tip 1: Single is not a status. It's a word that best describes a person who is strong enough to live and enjoy life without depending on others. Being single doesn't mean no one wants you; it just means that God is busy writing your love story.
Philippians 1:6: Only God can complete you.

Relationship Tip 2: Let haters talk. People are like music; some speak the truth, and others are just noise. You will never be truly happy if you continuously hold on to what people say about your relationship. Love hard and move on!
James 3:16: Some people are jealous.

Relationship Tip 3: It's unfortunate that some women prefer crazy over kindness. Instead of gentlemen, they'd rather have *mental*-men. Stop being thirsty for Mr. Wrong, and thank God for Mr. Right.
Song of Solomon 5:16: You deserve the best.

Relationship Tip 4: You are perfect in your imperfections, happy in your pain, strong in your weaknesses, and beautiful in your own way because you are you. Your love is like a

crayon: It may not be their favorite color, but know someday they will wish they had you to complete their picture.
Deuteronomy 28:13: I will no longer settle for less than I deserve.

Relationship Tip 5: It's funny how the people who hurt you the most are the ones who swore they never would. Sometimes it's better to just move on instead of being the only one who's willing fix things. Cheating is a choice, not a mistake.
1 Corinthians 4:2: Be faithful.

Relationship Tip 6: Cheating on a person who loves *you* is deeper than people realize. It can destroy their outlook on love, their future relationships, and their peace within themselves. It is like throwing away a diamond and picking up a rock — *your* loss.
Proverbs 11:1: God hates a cheater.

Relationship Tip 7: You can't make anyone love you. You're waiting on them to love you back and calling it faith, when the truth is you're just wasting your time. If people can't come up to your level of standards, don't go down to theirs. Just wave from the balcony and be done with it.
Isaiah 13:2: Protect your standards.

Relationship Tip 8: Ladies, love is like a card game: get rid of the *jokers*, guard your *heart*, set a *diamond* standard, and wait on God to send you a *king*.
Psalm 27:14: Serve God and be patient.

Relationship Tip 9: Stop trying to force people to love you. Be yourself. Loving you should be a wonderful privilege, not just an obligation.
Song of Solomon 4:7: You are flawless.

Chapter 23

Relationship Tip 10: You can't place yourself in compromising situations that trigger your struggle and then think that God has failed you. It was *God* telling you not to go over there! God often removes a person from your life to protect your heart. Think about that before you go running after someone.
Proverbs 4:23: Guard your heart and take it *slow*, or your heart will have to fight to let go.

Relationship Tip 11: Don't chase people. Chase God, be you, do your own thing, work hard, and the right people who belong in your life will come to you and stay.
1 Samuel 30:6: Never sweat it or regret it. Just encourage yourself and forget it.

Relationship Tip 12: How can you give anybody your heart if it's already with another? Until your heart is completely available, you're really unavailable. Just because your body's in a relationship doesn't mean your heart is.
Proverbs 6:5: Make sure you free yourself first.

Relationship Tip 13: Sex won't make a man love you, and a baby won't make him stay. Sometimes you have to forget what *you* want and remember what God says you *deserve*.
Proverbs 1:31: You deserve the *best*.

Relationship Tip 14: Commitment doesn't mean sticking to one person forever. It means *committing* in a relationship with someone even though you have lots of options. "Your mind is like your bed. You must *commit* to making it up every day and be careful who you let in it." – TD Brown
Colossians 2:8: Don't let anyone deceive you.

Relationship Tip 15: There are many people who will try to stand between you and what you want. Don't let yourself be one of those people. Close your legs, not your mind!
Proverbs 19:8: Show love for yourself. Use common sense.

Relationship Tip 16: If the dating relationship isn't working, don't get married thinking it'll improve. All you'll do is just make breaking up expensive. You can't date wrong and expect to marry right.
Proverbs 3:5: Pray and allow God to lead you.

Relationship Tip 17: A real man will accept you and your baggage, then love you enough to help you unpack. But, ladies, don't expect your partner to always know what you want him to do; he can't read your mind. If you want it, *say* it.
Proverbs 30:7-9: Communicate your needs.

Relationship Tip 18: So, stop telling all your business and comparing your partner to your Ex. Either you is with the Ex or with the next, you can't have both chapters open. . If you keep telling everyone about what your EX did to you, how they were wrong and how you're better without them; you're not over them ....If you keep letting them string you along, they'll just tie you up forever...
1 Corinthians 15:33-Some people you know need to become-the people you knew!

Relationship Tip 19: A true relationship is when you can tell each other anything and everything, no secrets and no lies.
Ephesians 4:15: Love your mate enough to tell him the truth.

Relationship Tip 20: Love is like the sun. In dark times it appears to be absent, but it's still shining and soon to come

Chapter 23

back to light your day. Get close enough to have fun, but don't get attached enough to get hurt.
Philippians 4:6: So *don't* rush it!

Relationship Tip 21: Relationships are about being selfless. So if you get with somebody who knows you already *have* someone, that's *selfish*! That's a dead-end relationship. If they'll cheat with you, they'll cheat on you, because they *don't* understand covenant.
Matthew 10:16: Be humble, but *wise*.

Relationship Tip 22: Appreciate those who love you. Help those who need you. Forgive those who hurt you. Forget those who leave you, and don't allow the enemy to confuse being lonely with raging harmones.
Song of Solomon 4:9: If stolen, it's hard to get your heart back.

Relationship Tip 23: Never be so busy trying to get to the *next* relationship that you never take time to get over the *last* one, or the *next* may end up like the *last*! If you're not over the *last* relationship, you need to heal first, or the next relationship won't *last*.
Proverbs 18:24, MSG: Some people are seasonal; move on.

Relationship Tip 24: Flirting while in a relationship is highly disrespectful, and while it may seem harmless, it can be very hurtful to the person who loves you. Don't take your relationship for granted, then lose it and wish you would've treated it better.
Ecclesiastes Chp. 7:Keep it real. Never take anything for granted.

Relationship Tip 25: Never let a fool kiss you or kiss a fool yourself. Not everyone who has passion for you is God sent. There's a big difference between whom we love, whom we settle for, and whom we're meant for.

Mark 14:45: Some people have hidden agendas.

Dedication

To my friend, partner, and darling wife, Tammy, a woman who demonstrates the qualities and principles of a virtuous woman. Your love, respect, support, and confidence in me over many years of marriage have helped me to understand the gift and essence of a virtuous woman.

To my beloved daughters, Laprecious, Renee, and Rhonda, to whom I have dedicated my life to being a mortal father and mentor with the hope that they will become the quality of woman as their mother and someday be a wife of noble worth to a God-fearing man.

To my beloved sons, Tony Jr. and Jonathan, two young men who constantly display the character of their father. May you continue to follow God and pursue your dreams.

To my mother, Bernice, who showed me so much love throughout my childhood and even to this day. I thank you for pushing me to be the man God created me to be.

And to all the women who are in pursuit of their purpose in God. For many years, you have been victims of cultural, economic, social, and spiritual oppression. May this book aid you in discovering and experiencing the freedom of equality, dignity, and fulfillment that God has in store for you.

Acknowledgments

I realize that every accomplishment in life is a result of the contributions of many individuals who both directly and indirectly shared their talents, gifts, and wisdom with us all. I appreciate all of the women at Threshing Floor Christian Fellowship Church who have applied these principles throughout the years and have shared feedback from their relationships. Most of all, I am grateful to the Creator of both men and women, who has blessed us with all of our gifts.

About the Author

*P*astor Tony Brown is a multigifted husband, father, certified relationship coach, national speaker, lecturer, educator, relationship advisor, entrepreneur, and anointed pastor who addresses critical issues affecting the full range of social, political, and spiritual development. The central theme of his message is purpose, healing, development, and how to maximize relationships.

Pastor Brown is the founder and senior pastor of Threshing Floor Christian Fellowship (TFCF) and president-founder of Macon-A-Change Youth Empowerment Center. He is known for his cutting edge, crisp simplicity, and the practical principles of his sermons. His numerous accomplishments encompass both the secular and the spiritual realms. During his twenty-three years of naval service, he received many awards, including six U.S. Navy achievement medals. He has reached the masses through his travel to over twenty different countries and through numerous outreach ministries. He has been acknowledged and awarded by local, state, and federal agencies for his outstanding volunteer work and consistent work with youth, jails, and nursing homes.

Pastor T. D. Brown is anointed, and his skillful exegetical handling of the Scriptures, along with his personal and

About The Author

down-to-earth approach to the gospel, has drawn followers locally, throughout the United States, and abroad. He travels the world sharing the good news of Jesus Christ. His duties are more far-reaching than what has been listed here. He lists his greatest of all accomplishments as being happily married to Tammy Griffin-Brown for twenty years. They serve as relationship experts and a model couple to pastors and ministry leaders in several states.

Shout-out! *To all the women reading this book, who aren't interested in being "The Other Woman", "Side Chick", Friends with benefits", "or the "Jump Off"...You Rock!*

CPSIA information can be obtained at www.ICGtesting.com
Printed in the USA
LVOW12s2210021013

355207LV00001B/27/P